WHAT THE
QUEEN
SAID TO ME...

BY CHILLI BRENER

UNICORN

First published by Unicorn,
an imprint of the Unicorn Publishing Group LLP, 2017
101 Wardour Street
London
W1F 0UG

www.unicornpublishing.org

© Chilli Brener

ISBN 978-1-910787-51-9

10 9 8 7 6 5 4 3 2 1

Cover design and typeset by Vivian@Bookscribe

Printed and bound in India by Imprint Press

CONTENTS

> *Please do not contact any contributor without prior consent from Chilli Brener. Thank you.*

Introduction

My name is Chilli Brener and I started writing professionally at the ripe age of forty something. Some rather dark poetry and a few articles in some old magazines was about my limit. It was most certainly not on my agenda to write a non-fiction book.

Sometimes though things happen, whether small or big, and your life takes an unexpected road. An incredibly small thing happened to me one day back in 2012 which took me on this incredibly long and wonderful journey. In that moment life changed and I was most definitely driving up a road I never knew existed.

You see, I caught the tail end of a news interview on a TV that I wasn't even watching. At this precise moment I just happened to walk past.

The interviewer was with a gentleman who was talking about his meeting with Queen Elizabeth II.

"What The Queen said to me…" is a book inspired by that news interview.

The gentleman had just been asked the final question: "Can you remember what The Queen said to you?" It caught my attention and I was interested in what his answer was. Strangely, it was not so much what he said but how he said it that tweaked my interest. It struck me that he seemed a little petulant. His chippy response of: "Well, of course I can. It is an experience I will never forget!" really got me thinking.

This small and seemingly insignificant comment which, let's face it, I could quite easily have missed whilst carrying out my mundane household chores, got my rusty and old, but still relatively creative, cogs whirring!

I figured that if this gentleman remembered every single word, then surely other people who have met The Queen would remember too! After all, it's a very personal and, more often than not, a once-in-a-lifetime experience. The Queen is relatively inaccessible. For her to utter a few words only to you for that one small moment in time is an experience many ordinary folk don't get the opportunity to have. It must be pretty special! So the idea for this book was born.

Contributors were actually quite hard to find but when I did find them they all said pretty much the same thing – "Yes, I remember exactly what The Queen said" – and so the process started.

I started putting the feelers out to find stories from people who had actually spoken with The Queen. It proved rather difficult – there were many people who had been in The Queen's company but not many that had shared words. I came across only two people who had stories to tell. Well, it was a start.

Ultimately, the idea for this book is to document – not just for the here and now – but, for history, the words and phrases this lady, our Queen for over sixty years, has said to many people. She has brought a smile to many a face and my aim is to get across a tiny snippet of her personality and sense of humour to those who have not been fortunate enough to have met her. I knew the book would have to have a photograph of the storyteller too. Seeing the person that told the story speaks a thousand words.

All the stories are written from the point of view of the person involved and always in their own words. The contributor sets the scene, tells the story and then sums up their personal impression of The Queen. It is as simple as that. I am not talking about vast conversations or unearthing some great secret. I am talking about one or two sentences; little chats and anecdotes, personal stories which have affected people's lives. Ordinary folk, some we have heard of and some we have not, but people who have had an extraordinary experience. Without a book like this these people would not have had their stories told!

"What The Queen said to me..." is my debut. It is a very big and important part of my life. It has taken much work and has been so very time consuming. I have met and spent a lot of time with each contributor, bar one and each person was recommended to me. I felt it was incredibly important to see the body language and the facial expressions and to hear the slight changes to the tone of the voice or the laughter brought on by the recollection of a funny part to the story. Passion in people comes out in many ways and I needed to feel that passion. All the little idiosyncrasies that crop up when one is telling an interesting or well loved story are as important to the story as the story itself.

Research for most of my stories came after the initial interview. For instance, getting all the facts and dates right, making sure names and titles are accurate and events did actually take place as described. Researching historical facts has been wonderful, particularly in looking at The Queen's Watermen or the role of Mace bearers, the Royal British Legion or MENCAP and how many investitures there are and the differences in meaning of OBEs, CBEs, KBEs etc.

Getting published was the biggie. I won't go into details but I would say that hearing a talk by a rather successful author stating he had received 300 rejection letters, twice, really inspired me. Whenever I had a down moment I thought of him and his self belief. That is why *"What The Queen said to me..."* is here now.

When I interviewed people for the book it struck me early on that most folk would remember every word The Queen had muttered to them. It also struck me how sad it was that most of these stories have been told in the past to family and friends but then been put away in the little box of memories that rarely gets opened again unless somebody randomly asks, "What did happen when you met The Queen, Grandma?"

Some of the older stories were told with the contributor's memory working overtime. The details of the why's and where's and when's were struggled with and the human auto correct was set to extreme. Come the point in the interview when I asked "So what did The Queen say to you...?" there was not a lot of thinking or struggling or straining. It was very much a straight and precise answer, remembered in a very light way like that moment was always sitting at the surface of the buried story. I should probably take this opportunity to apologise to readers on behalf of my contributors – if any of the facts are wrong then please do forgive, memories can be tricky sometimes.

It is important to get across to you, the reader, that each interview seemed to awaken a soul, revive a lost moment in time. By sharing these anecdotes not only does one get a rare glimpse into the very guarded personality of The Queen but one also gets to acknowledge a story told and shared – a story never to be hidden in the lost box of memories again.

So many different types of anecdote. Each one written with its own integrity at its heart. The way the story was told by its owner is the way it is written in this book. No frills or embellishments.

To know that these stories have a little place in history gives me such a lovely warm feeling. From the bottom of my heart I want to thank everyone that has taken the time to tell me their story and to thank *you* for reading them.

Long Live The Queen.

Chilli Brener

CHAPTER 1
Harold Walter Batten

WHO: Harold Walter Batten aka John Batten (Deceased)
WHERE: London
WHEN: 1930s and 1940s
WHY: Anecdotal contributions

The following are three short anecdotal stories recollected by Chris Batten, John's son.

"My father, John Batten, had trained as a tailor in the early 1930s. He worked for a company in London called McDougall & Sons. They were highland outfitters. John worked on the sales side of the business and it was his job to visit the customers to take their measurements. His boss called him in one day and said, 'I want you to go to this house in Piccadilly.' He gave John the address and added, 'They have two young daughters and they want them measured for their first kilts.'

John, Chris and Dorothy Batten, 1946

John went to the address he had been given. He knocked on the door and waited. The royal valet, Tom Jerome, opened the door and showed him in. Suddenly, two young girls appeared. The elder one, aged around seven years old, was called Lilibet and the younger one, aged around four, was called Margaret Rose. Lilibet was very formal and said to John, 'How do you do.' She politely shook his hand.

Margaret Rose, however, being three years younger, pootled around, lifted up her skirt, and said, 'Look! I'm wearing my new knickers!' Lilibet was not very pleased with her younger sister and told her off. John suddenly realised these were the daughters of The Duke and Duchess of York, who later became King George VI and Queen Elizabeth. Lilibet, the little girl who had shaken his hand, would later become Queen Elizabeth II. "

"*My father was a great man. When I was young, I think around 1946, my father took me to Buckingham Palace. He had had a career move and had joined a company called Thresher & Glenny. Thresher & Glenny had a Royal appointment at the time and, one day, it was my father who was invited to measure King George VI for a suit. He took me. I was thrilled to bits. The same King's valet, Mr Jerome, greeted us at the back door of the palace. He took me into a room and told me to wait until my dad had finished measuring. Looking back, it was quite surreal. It was my first visit to Buckingham Palace and – I have to say – what an experience for a young chap like me. And what a privilege.* "

"*As I am talking about my father, John, I would like to include a great cartoon that was done of him back in 1946. It was created by the wartime cartoonist, William (Pat) Rooney. We think Pat may have worked for a while as a cartoonist with the 'New Yorker', but he also served with my father in the Supreme Headquarters Allied Expeditionary Force (SHAEF). John was one of a number of subjects, many associated in some way with the military, who were caricatured by Pat Rooney. John, a civilian, still worked for Thresher & Glenny, who provided tailored uniforms for the British Officers in the SHAEF.*"

CHAPTER 2

Victoria Baker

WHO: Victoria Baker
WHERE: Oxford
WHEN: March 1976
WHY: Official Opening of the Oxford County Council Offices

You'll have to bear with me as my memory isn't what it used to be. I'm ninety-seven, you know. Anyway, I will try hard to remember what happened.

I had a lovely little office, with no door, mind, in the cartography department of the Oxfordshire County Council. The chaps used to come down to me with their maps and ask me to produce or reproduce a certain part. I used to help make maps; that was my job and I loved it. I worked with what was like a mangle and used this machine to print off different sections of the map so the other cartographers could update buildings etc.

It was also my job to visit people who had applied for planning permission. There was not a part of Oxford that I didn't know and I did that job for over forty years. Like I said earlier, my memory lets me down. I mean it's forty years ago and it's a long time to go back and remember.

Victoria Baker

I recall the new offices which were being officially opened by The Queen were located in town next to the prison. New Road and Castle Street, I think; it was on a corner, anyhow. There was a fish shop underneath with a lot of fish swimming around. Funny how you remember such things.

Because I had worked there for so long I must have been coming up to retirement age and I think that's why they asked if I wanted to be included in the visit. Naturally I said yes, but there were a lot of my colleagues who said no.

I was very clothes-conscious in those days, so I decided to wear a nice fitting suit. I think Her Majesty wore blue. She always looks smart. Anyway, I was a bit worried I might fall over when I curtseyed, because I was a bit fat in those days! It was okay in the end though, and when The Queen spoke to me, which was only for a very short time, she seemed to know I was due to retire because she said...

WHAT THE QUEEN SAID TO ME ...

"How long have you worked here?"

My reply was simple. I said, "Forty years thereabouts. I'm due to retire."

The Queen then said something like, "Well, that's a long time. Well done." And then she moved on to the next person. It was over in a flash.

RIGHT: Victoria Baker and The Queen in Oxford

SUM THE QUEEN UP IN ONE PARAGRAPH:

"I have to say she really was lovely and she made you feel at home. She was nice, a bit aloof, but charming and lovely. She had a word for everybody even if it was short. I felt privileged to have met her. I think now, from what I see and read, she's much more relaxed and at one with everyone like she has mellowed. She was a little stoic in those days."

CHAPTER 3

Nellie Williams

WHO:	Nellie Williams
WHERE:	Royal Crescent, Bath
WHEN:	1977
WHY:	Walkabout for the Silver Jubilee

My name is Nellie. When I was a young girl my grandparents lived in Bath and we used to go and spend a lot of time with them in the holidays. To me it was a big throbbing city compared to the village I lived in, and I used to love and look forward very much to those Bath trips. My grandparents lived on Bathwick Hill which, if you know Bath, is the hill that leads to the university.

We would often venture downhill into town to visit various other family members. My aunt and my great grandmother, 'Little Great Granny' we called her, lived on the Royal Crescent in Bath – a wonderful sweeping arc of terraced Georgian townhouses built in the 1700s.

In 1977, as part of the Silver Jubilee Celebrations, The Queen was scheduled to do a walkabout, sort of a meet and greet on the Royal Crescent and there was no way our family was going to miss it. I was so excited.

Nellie Williams

Back then the Royal family were always featured on the news and in *Majesty Magazine* and it seemed to me that everyone had pictures of the Royal Family in their houses somewhere. I remember my grandmother had a photograph of The Queen Mother in her laundry room; it was a time and generation when people always stood up whenever they heard the National Anthem. Now before I tell you what happened in the Royal Crescent when I finally met The Queen, I need to fill you in with a little back story.

As children, my brother and I used to go to a lovely nursery school and, like most schools, often we had day trips. Some of these trips were quite random. Once we went wandering down the road to see someone's garden of daffodils. Another time we went to see the chickens at the local chicken farm; it was not about learning about the chickens, it was standing at the fence and looking in. But, every year we would go on a special day trip. I cannot remember exactly how many years we went on this day trip but it was a family event which my brother, who was older than me, also attended. I think we went at least three or four times.

The trip was always to Windsor Great Park where we would have a lovely picnic and watch The Queen and the procession as they went from Windsor to the races at Ascot. I thought it was magical; all the children would be in their school uniforms with little red berets for the girls and little red caps for the boys. As The Queen went past we would all be waving frantically at her with flags, red caps and berets.

With that back story in mind I will take you back to Bath and the summer of 1977. I was eight and standing with my brother and his cuddly koala and my grandfather, a strong, stoic man. The Queen was walking along and saying hello to lots of people and she was getting closer and closer. I could hear her: "Good afternoon." "How are you." "Nice to meet you" etc. She spoke to many many people including my Grandfather to whom she said, "Good afternoon". He was very gracious and calm as one would expect.

They had a short chitchat and then she got to me!!

I, in my high pitched, squeaky, fast, excited beyond belief, urgent voice, squealed "Do ya... d... do you remember me????" The sentence spewed out as if it were just one word and it was incredibly uncouth and so high pitched. But in my urgency I continued squealing. "I... I used to stand in Windsor Great Park and wave my red beret at you, do ya remember, do you??"

My grandfather was mortified with embarrassment, stiff upper lip and all that. And my poor brother, clutching his cuddly koala bear, just wishing the ground would swallow him, or me, either would have done. For me it was so exciting to be actually seeing this amazing woman; the lady we had seen in the newspapers and on the television. The one that we used to wave at with our red hats. I had to ask her, I had to. I was eight!

And then came The Queen's reply and she said very slowly, with a lovely smile across her face...

WHAT THE QUEEN SAID TO ME . . .

"Well, yes, I think I do."

I was like, yeah, ok she did, wow, I knew it, cool. I was so chuffed and so glad I asked. Her response totally and utterly made my day, my week, my holiday. Afterwards it was great telling my friends what I had done in the holidays. "Oh, you know, I met the Queen."

The Queen was the most famous person in the world to me. And do you know, I don't know if she did or didn't recognise me that day but she had the forethought to think that it would mean a lot to me, this eight-year-old girl in front of her. I have been a massive fan ever since.

Nellie as an eight-year-old child with her brother just before the royal meeting

SUM THE QUEEN UP IN ONE PARAGRAPH:

"As an eight year old, The Queen just seemed like somebody that my grandparents knew. Like someone's grandma. Happy and comfortable. Iconic but not like a flashy film star. Now, I see her Majesty as this amazing lady who has lived through so much and seen so much. Let's face it she wasn't destined to be Queen, was she? I think she has done a fantastic job and hasn't changed at all. I'm glad I met her and I am glad I said what I said because her reply not only made my day but in my eyes it also made her human."

CHAPTER 4

Brigadier Malcolm Page

WHO:	Brigadier Malcolm Page
WHERE:	Bicester
WHEN:	1978
WHY:	State Visit to the Ministry of Defence Depot (MOD)

I met The Queen at a State Visit to the Ministry of Defence Depot (MOD) in Bicester in 1978. I was Brigadier and Her Majesty was Colonel-in-Chief of The Royal Army Ordnance Corps (RAOC). My role was to show her around the depot and to escort her throughout the day.

We spoke about the bomb disposal suits that were due to be sent to Canada later that year ahead of her visit. She named a locomotive on-site called *Conductor*, which is actually a rank in the RAOC. At the end of the visit The Queen said…

WHAT THE QUEEN SAID TO ME …

"Thank you so much for a wonderful day."

Brigadier Malcolm Page

Unexpectedly, a little while later I received a formal letter from The Queen's Private Secretary thanking me personally. I have it in my photo album. I was also given a commemorative bowl (*above*), commissioned specially for that day.

Malcolm has another story. He was President of the Henley & Peppard branch of the Royal British Legion when this event took place. It was 6 November 1998, a lovely crisp but sunny day and the opening of the River & Rowing Museum in Henley-on-Thames.

WHERE: River & Rowing Museum, Henley-on-Thames
WHEN: 6 November 1998
WHY: Grand Opening of the Museum

I had just taken over as President of the Royal British Legion a few months before The Queen's visit to Henley. I had the bright idea that we could form a guard of honour for Her Majesty as she came up from the jetty to the entrance of the museum. She would have left Phyllis Court by launch and on her approach to the landing site, she would see around sixty of us lining the route.

We all assembled at the Salisbury Conservative Club in Henley. They included the County Standard Bearer and the Women's Section County Standard Bearer, our own and two or three other Standard Bearers. We also had one chap called Bill Stone [William Frederick "Bill" Stone], who was an uninvited but very welcome guest. He was about eighty-nine at the time, one of the last surviving veterans of World War I. He had been a stoker and he joined the Royal Navy in about October 1918, I think. He sadly died in 2009 at the age of 109.

Bill didn't belong to our Royal British Legion branch but he didn't want to miss this great occasion so he just turned up, spirited to the last. What an amazing man. He chuckled and told me that he had told The Queen that he is as old as her mother! Unfortunately I don't know what her reply to him was.

When the time came to leave, I got up and said, "Come on, then. Let's go." Some of the group, a little perturbed, asked, "Are we not going to march then?" I suddenly felt very proud of them and so said, "Yes, let's do just that." So, for the first time in thirty years I got people to fall in, and we started marching to the River & Rowing Museum.

Malcolm with The Queen at MOD Bicester in 1978

We all lined up and waited for The Queen to arrive on the Royal Barge, *Windrush*. She came ashore and Allan Follett, the Mayor of Henley-on Thames at the time, guided Her Majesty up to where we were. Allan then introduced The Queen to me saying, "This is Brigadier Malcolm Page, President of the Royal British Legion."

WHAT THE QUEEN SAID TO ME...

"*And which standards are these?*"

I told her about the various standards, and she seemed both very interested and knowledgeable. I was just about to introduce two acquaintances, Mac and Ann, when The Queen spotted some children on the other side of the walkway and, gleaming, she said, "Oh! Some children." Then, distracted, she promptly turned around to see the children. Mac, very disappointed, quickly drew his hand back from what he thought was an imminent handshake. Ann? Well, she didn't have a chance. Sad to say, but it didn't go quite as I had planned in my head for either of them.

SUM THE QUEEN UP IN ONE PARAGRAPH:

"*On both occasions, she really did want to speak to as many people as she could. She always had something polite to say to them. She is always professional but it was fascinating to see how much more experience she had in the latter meeting some twenty years later. She is a wonderful woman.*"

CHAPTER 5
Chris Batten

WHO: Chris Batten

WHERE: Muttrah Harbour, Oman

WHEN: 1979

WHY: Evening Reception to watch the Royal Marine Band Beat the Retreat

It was back in 1979 when I was working in Muscat, Oman. My wife, Madella, and I had been invited to a reception on board the Royal Yacht *Britannia* for Queen Elizabeth II's visit to Oman. The Queen and Prince Phillip had invited The Sultan of Oman, Qaboos bin Said Al Said, his ministers and an array of guests on board to watch the Beating Retreat.

Madella and I made our way to Muttrah, the commercial harbour of Greater Muscat. We showed our invitations, went aboard and approached the receiving line which included The Queen and Prince Philip, the Duke of Edinburgh.

The British Ambassador was making the introductions. I shook hands with Queen Elizabeth, who didn't actually speak to me at this point, and then I shook hands with Prince Philip. He said to me, "I know your boss in Bahrain. You work for a company that has a funny name. It's something like sharafat e can yea?"

I told him he had it very nearly right, and that it was Sharikat Fanniya Omaniya

Chris Batten

(Muscat) LLC, the technical company of Oman. He chuckled. This brief conversation broke the ice and it was the start of a very nice and relaxed evening. We all went in and there was some banter with the Royal Navy Commander, Graham Creedy, about a lack of beer on board. Not only was Commander Creedy in charge of supplies on board, he also happened to be an old school friend of mine. I found out from Graham that only Royal Navy wardroom drinks are served at receptions like this, and beer was most definitely off the menu!

Earlier, The Queen had hosted a dinner party for the Sultan and his cabinet in the saloon of the Royal Yacht *Britannia*. The evening reception was held so we could mingle with the ministers and watch the Royal Marine Band Beat the Retreat on the Muttrah quayside.

It was quite amusing because at this point the Duke of Edinburgh came over and said to my wife, "Why don't you come up onto the boat deck with me because we will get a much better view of the Beating Retreat up there?" She disappeared with him and I stayed and watched the Beating Retreat with The Queen, the Sultan, his ministers and the various guests. It really was spectacular and the sun was setting. I was feeling confident and we all started to mingle.

Just before the retreat started, The Queen came over to join our group. It was rather good timing and she started to recite a story. This is what she said…

WHAT THE QUEEN SAID TO ME...

"*A very funny thing happened to me earlier today. We went on a visit to a stadium that was full of schoolchildren from the English speaking school here, and the Sultan insisted that I went in his car. It was a very nice limousine of some kind.*

It was rather funny because we went down a slight hill into the stadium which had a small ramp at the bottom. We went at a speed that was not slow and all of a sudden there was an almighty noise and screech. I wondered what on earth had happened!
It turned out that the bottom of this lovely car had grounded and scraped over the ramp making the terrible racket. They had gone too fast and hadn't actually checked that the car could clear the ramp as it entered the stadium. It was rather amusing!"

At this moment, The Queen burst into a giggle, almost like a little girl! I found it such a lovely laugh and, of course, her laughing made everyone else laugh too.

SUM THE QUEEN UP IN ONE PARAGRAPH:

"*She is very human and very lively.*
The Queen has such a lovely laugh too."

CHAPTER 6
Mike Read

WHO: Mike Read

WHERE: Buckingham Palace, St. Paul's Cathedral, Birdcage Walk and The Royal Albert Hall

WHEN: 1979, 1982, 1988, 2004

WHY: An informal meeting after a charity event and a reading at The Prince's Trust Rock Gala

Not long after I joined Radio One, the UN proclaimed 1979 as International Year of the Child with the aim of promoting awareness and encouraging the protection of children's rights. During that year there were many celebrations worldwide, one of which took place at Buckingham Palace. The event was a most exceptional and atmospheric spectacle with over 10,000 children from many nations taking part. The Mall was literally jammed from one end to the other with flaming torches and raised voices and dozens of musicians were positioned in the Buckingham Palace courtyard.

I was conducting the proceedings from a constructed stage around the Victoria Memorial in front of the palace. Cliff Richard performed a few carols and graciously invited me to join him on a couple of the songs. Meanwhile, The Queen, accompanied by her son, Prince Charles, came out onto the balcony to the delight of the thousands of children.

The band began to play. The choir began to sing and the flaming torches started to give

Mike Read

off enough smoke to warrant a weather warning! I began to notice that the band and the choir were getting increasingly out of sync without any tangible or audible reason. Certainly not as far as I could see. The further apart they drifted, the more painful it became. There was little I could do about it though, from my elevated position on the stage and being out of time isn't, as far as I know, a treasonable offence.

The rest of the evening went off without a hitch and, after I'd made a closing speech thanking The Queen and Prince Charles, an official from Buckingham Palace came out and ushered Cliff and myself into the palace. I remember saying to Cliff, "I bet a corgi comes in first," a tongue-in-cheek predication that proved to be one hundred per cent correct!

After our initial introduction, The Queen's voice changed slightly. There was a hint of guilt in her voice, as she went rather *sotto voce* to confess…

WHAT THE QUEEN SAID TO ME…

"I think I might have caused a bit of a problem."

Immediately realising what she meant, I said, "Yes. I think you did, Ma'am."

"Oh, you noticed. I was only wafting the smoke away."

The reason the choir had been so out of sync with the band was because of the smoke from the flaming torches. In order to see through the smoke, The Queen had started to waft it away. In doing this, the kids in the choir – who all had had their eyes peeled on The Queen and Prince Charles on the balcony – were singing in time with The Queen's wafting hand movements, rather than keeping in time with the band.

"I think it was all my fault," she continued.
"I think they thought I was conducting them."

It was an amusing and lovely meeting. I went to tell my mother all about it. Needless to say, she was thrilled!

The second meeting I had with The Queen took place at The Royal Albert Hall in 1988. This was a Prince's Trust Rock Gala and I had been invited to do a reading. Now I find hosting, compering and singing relatively easy, but reading a lengthy and serious piece on the plight of children was a different matter – there was no room for mistakes in this kind of situation. Fortunately, I completed the reading without any hiccups and, when the event was over, I met The Queen again. I very much doubt that she watched Top of the Pops, but she had been suitably primed.

WHAT THE QUEEN SAID TO ME...

"We are very grateful to you for making it here. I hear you had to dash away from Top of the Pops to get here in time."

I smiled, as you do, and said it wasn't a problem. We had a photograph taken for posterity.

Of course, The Queen had been told that I had had to rush over at breakneck speed from BBC Television Centre in order to get to The Royal Albert Hall on time, but it is extraordinary that she is able to absorb and retain possibly dozens of facts and figures about the many individuals that she is likely to meet. I had noticed that nobody had prompted her in the moments before our meeting. Extraordinary.

WHERE: Birdcage Walk, The South Bank
WHEN: 2004
WHY: A very impromptu meeting

The third time I met The Queen it was a very informal and impromptu moment.

Early one morning just after "I'm a Celebrity, Get Me Out of Here!" had finished, I was heading down to the South Bank to appear on a breakfast television programme.

Driving west along Birdcage Walk, the traffic was halted and a number of motorcycle outriders appeared and stopped just in front of me. They were obviously waiting for a car to catch up with them. I assumed, as you would, that it was a member of the Royal Family or a visiting royal, and I wasn't disappointed. The said car appeared and temporarily pulled up right next to me. It had to wait momentarily for more outriders from the escort to catch up. The window was down on that car and I was in a convertible with my roof off and my window down.

I looked across and it was The Queen. There was no time for formalities.

I simply smiled and said, "Morning".

"Morning," replied the monarch, a second before her limousine moved off.

There wasn't even time to add, "Your Majesty."

It was a rather surreal moment. We were only a yard away from each other. My mother was thrilled when I told her this story and she pleaded, "Tell me more. Tell me more." I told her there was no more. That was it!

WHERE:	St Paul's Cathedral
WHEN:	1982
WHY:	No spoken words took place at this event, just a look and sheer embarrassment!

There was another occasion. This was in 1982. I technically spoke to The Queen, but, she didn't speak to me. Not that she was meant to, however, she did give me a suitably admonishing look. In another era I may have ended up in the tower but in this age of comparative reason, she just gave me the very unimpressed eye.

I had just arrived in London after a night crossing by sea and I still hadn't quite got my "land-legs". I had raced across town as I was scheduled to do a reading at St. Paul's Cathedral for the BBC's Diamond Jubilee. This was a daunting prospect in itself, but the tiredness and wobbly legs made it even more so. I passed rows and rows of famous

BBC faces from my childhood it was a very special experience. I felt privileged to be one of two chosen readers to represent the BBC at such a momentous occasion. We navigated the walk without mishap and eventually I peeled off to my lectern.

The Queen, Prince Philip and other members of the Royal Family were just three or four feet in front of me. Everybody in St. Paul's, including Her Majesty The Queen and the Royal Family, were standing. Watching.

And then the most embarrassing moment of my life occurred. So embarrassing I didn't even turn red – I went white!

There was a seat right next to my lectern. A very inviting seat. I was so relieved to get to my position because of my sea legs, I sat down!

Seriously… What was I thinking?

It was a moment, only a moment, but my bottom had touched the seat. I suddenly felt everybody's eyes on me. Too late to save myself from being strung up on the gallows at Tyburn, my brain told my body that something was wrong. It said, "The Queen, and everybody else, is standing, and you, idiot child, have plonked yourself into a chair in front of her nose!"

Any honours, riches and lands that she may have been considering bestowing upon me for this exceptional role, were disappearing into the sunset as I rose slowly and, I hoped, imperceptibly. I unfolded myself and stared at the floor. I thought it best not to catch her eye.

I've thought since that, had I been more quick-witted that day, I could have made it look like I was saying a quick prayer. But I wasn't and I didn't.

No one said anything. They didn't have to. Her Majesty said it all with her eyes.

Despite the treasonable start, the reading was fine. I asked my mother and my girlfriend, my biggest critics, if the reading came across well and thankfully the seal of approval was forthcoming. That made me feel a lot happier but it was, and remains, *one of the most embarrassing moments of my life.*

SUM UP THE QUEEN IN ONE PARAGRAPH:

"Most of us have only ever known The Queen as our monarch. She has been ever-present, has had to keep pace with an ever-changing world and adapt with each era. Despite the dramatic changes in technology, attitudes, expectations, education, human rights and travel since she came to the throne almost sixty-five years ago, she has continued to reign with dignity, wisdom and decorum.
I am proud to be living in a country with a monarchy and not a republic. The Queen is a magnificent figurehead, ably supported by Prince Philip with his rather mischievous sense of humour and Prince Charles, whose work for young people via the Prince's Trust is incredible. May I add that I think Prince William and Prince Harry are also terrific role models when you consider what those two boys have been through."

CHAPTER 7
Sophie Kyriakides

WHO: Sophie Kyriakides
WHERE: Windsor Great Park
WHEN: Late 1980s
WHY: Horse riding event

This is probably going to be the shortest story in this book but when I was a teenager I took part in show jumping and horse riding events. Riding horses was my love and I entered many competitions. It just so happened that I was taking part in a sponsored ride in the Windsor Great Park way back in the late 1980s. I happened to be doing a jump just in front of where The Queen was standing. I proudly completed the jump, cleanly and with no mistakes. A second later I heard the very unique voice of The Queen. Quite loudly and with energy she shouted…

WHAT THE QUEEN SAID TO ME…

"Good jump!!"

That was it, simple and to the point.

Sophie Kyriakides

It is funny because when I was being interviewed, Chilli asked, "Do you remember anything else that you did that year – anything?"

I wracked my brains and could think of nothing. It is a very fond memory that has always stuck in my mind. It felt really nice that The Queen had actually noticed that I had done something well and had decided to share it with me and the people she was with. A short and proud moment.

CHAPTER 8

Flora Preston

WHO:	Flora Preston
WHERE:	Shire Hall, Shinfield Park
WHEN:	2 April 1982
WHY:	Official opening of Shire Hall, part of the Berkshire County Council offices

1982 was a hard year for The Queen and when I met Her Majesty I could tell she looked a little uneasy. This visit happened to be taking place on the day of the breakout of the Falklands War. I knew that Prince Andrew was flying a helicopter in the conflict and as a mother myself I would imagine that this only added to the stress The Queen was under. As a result of this announcement The Queen was late, but she did arrive, she didn't cancel, she did not let anyone down and she did carry out her duties that day in a professional, committed and interested way.

I was the head teacher of Beenham Primary School in Berkshire at the time of the Royal visit. The county council offices were being officially opened by The Queen and I was lucky enough to be asked to escort Her Majesty around part of the building – Shire Hall. A number of the local schools were invited to put up exhibitions of their children's artwork to decorate the hall and I have to say the artwork all looked wonderful. Each

Flora Preston

school's artwork stayed for a while and was then replaced with another school's work and so it went on. Beenham School was lucky because our school's artwork was being exhibited in the days running up to the Royal opening and so fortunately I was invited to the event, along with a number of the Year Five and Six children.

On Saturday, 2 April 1982, we stood primed, and we waited, and waited. The reason for her lateness soon became obvious as the news seeped out about the conflict. I was introduced to Her Majesty and we walked around the exhibition together. We all understood and accepted the delay, after all it was maybe only an hour or so. When The Queen did arrive she was very elegant. We talked in general about the hall and The Queen asked many questions about the artwork. It really was a pleasant exchange. The bit I particularly remember though, and found rather interesting, was when she asked about some of the cushions in the exhibit.

WHAT THE QUEEN SAID TO ME...

"Did the boys make the cushions too?"

She asked with a slight curiosity in her voice.

I told her, "Yes, the boys did make the cushions as well as the girls and, in fact, I think the boys were definitely more creative and did a better job than most of the girls."

I went on to tell her that the boys were treated in exactly the same way as the girls in the school and visa versa. The Queen seemed to be quite interested and in agreement with this.

SUM UP THE QUEEN IN ONE PARAGRAPH:

"*Oh, The Queen was charming and engaging – in spite of the circumstances and her obvious strain over the Falkland's situation – obvious to me anyway as I could feel it and see it in her face – Her Majesty carried on with the day and her duties totally as normal. She was very professional. I would like to add that the Lady in Waiting was also very elegant, charming and kind too. An experience I shall not forget and remember with fondness.*"

"*I did sort of meet The Queen once before, many many years before. It was when King George VI and Queen Elizabeth came to open the Empire Exhibition at Bellahouston Park in Glasgow on 3 May 1938.*

The Royal couple walked around the exhibition with their two daughters Princess Elizabeth and Princess Margaret. This walkabout followed the King's speech at Ibrox.

My mother took my sister and me to the exhibition. We were of a similar age to the two royal Princesses, about ten and twelve. The four of us were in very close proximity and we all smiled at each other. Funny how I remember that moment – I doubt The Queen does."

King George VI and Queen Elizabeth at The Empire Exhibition in 1938.
(Photo courtesy of House for an Artlover Heritage Centre)

*The Princesses inspecting the view
from the Tower
Picture: Courtesy of The Scotsman*

*Right: Princess Elizabeth as a child at the Empire Exhibition.
(Picture courtesy* The Scotsman*)*

CHAPTER 9
Richard Goddard

WHO: Richard Goddard, Secretary of the Henley Royal Regatta 1975–2006
and Trustee of the River and Rowing Museum, Henley-on-Thames

WHERE: Henley-on-Thames

WHEN: April 1986

WHY: The Official Opening of the Henley Royal Regatta Headquarters

The wording on the plaque which The Queen was here to unveil went something like: "Henley Royal Regatta Headquarters opened by Her Majesty Queen Elizabeth II on such-and-such a date." We received communication back from the palace to say that The Queen would rather it not say "Her Majesty Queen Elizabeth II". She would prefer it to say "Her Majesty The Queen", as that was the form that she was now adopting so we sent the amended wording to the architect.

About a week before the visit and the unveiling, this huge piece of glass arrived, wonderfully engraved on the back, and it was fitted into place. Peter and I were not present when it was erected, but we decided to have a look at it in situ a day or two later. We both gasped in horror. It said: "Unveiled by Her Majesty Queen Elizabeth II" – the exact wording The Queen didn't want.

Peter Coni, Chairman of the Henley Royal Regatta, was in hysterics as he knew he was going to have to call the palace to confess the mistake. He rang promptly and

Richard Goddard

reluctantly explained what had happened. He apologised profusely, and he asked that if Her Majesty would unveil this one, we would have another one made and erected very soon afterwards saying something like: "A plaque very like this was unveiled by Her Majesty The Queen." The Palace called back and said not to worry. They had spoken to Her Majesty and it really didn't matter at all. We had every intention of having the plaque changed but it never was, and it is still sitting proudly in place today.

HER MAJESTY QUEEN ELIZABETH II
UNVEILED THIS PLAQUE ON THE 16TH OF APRIL 1986
TO COMMEMORATE THE OPENING OF THE HEADQUARTERS OF
HENLEY ROYAL REGATTA

Henley Royal Regatta plaque, still with the incorrect wording

On the day of the opening The Queen unveiled the plaque and pronounced Henley Royal Regatta Headquarters officially open. The Royal party walked down a line of about forty to fifty people, made up of Stewards of the Regatta, also known as the Governing Body. Peter Coni was picking people randomly to introduce to Her Majesty. He turned to The Queen, pointed to one particular chap and started to say, "Oh, and of course you will know…" At which point the Queen looked hard at this gentleman and cut Peter off with the words, "Good Gracious, Gerald! I didn't recognise you without the dog collar!"

The gentleman in question turned out to be the Bishop of London, The Right Reverend Gerald Ellison, who The Queen knew rather well. This sent everyone into fits of laughter and made for a very humorous visit indeed.

We continued and, after the unveiling, we all went into the committee room. It is a

Richard Goddard (back of head) with Peter Coni and The Queen outside Henley Royal Regatta Headquarters

double-height room and the architect was there to show and explain the plans of the building. I was standing behind The Queen and next to The Duke of Edinburgh. The Duke was looking around and suddenly spied some windows right at the top, in the corner of the room. He poked the architect, pointed and said, "How do you open those then? They have handles but are about twenty-five feet in the air." The chairman, Peter, butted in to answer and said, "It's a question, Sir, that we have been asking the architects for about three months!"

The Royal Party then proceeded downstairs into the basement where they boarded a launch lined on the deck by Queen's Watermen. It really did look amazing. The party enjoyed a short cruise downriver, just past Phyllis Court and back again. Their return brought the Royal Party through the lower deck level and up the stairs at the back of Regatta Headquarters. This led up to my flat. The flat was built specifically for the Regatta Secretary and looks out over the river. The Queen took it all in, looked at me and said of the flat...

WHAT THE QUEEN SAID TO ME...

"Oh! How charming! Doesn't it have such lovely views."

I replied, telling her how lucky I felt to have it as my home. That was it with regard to my conversation with The Queen but, being in her company for such a long time, and hearing so many other conversations was a great experience.

We carried on with the visit. On the way out of my flat we had to walk past a large collection of my books. I was with The Duke who had started to look at the titles. Making conversation, I said to him, "They are mainly books on heraldry, Sir."

He had a cheeky smile and said...

"Ummm ... What you want is something on pub signs!"

I replied, with the same cheeky smile, "Well, if you look just there, Sir, you will see some." He did chuckle and we shared a moment, but The Duke refrained from getting one of the books down to have a look.

The windows, top right and top left, in the Boardroom at Henley Royal Regatta.

WHERE: River and Rowing Museum
WHEN: 6 November 1998
WHY: The Official Opening of the River and Rowing Museum

The 6 November 1998, saw the Official Opening of the River and Rowing Museum in Henley-on-Thames. There was a mass of hundreds of people out that day.

I had no idea I was going to meet Her Majesty but when I got to the museum I was asked to be at the bottom of the stairs in the foyer area.

I waited patiently with a number of other people at the foot of the stairs and I positioned myself in line in order to be presented to The Queen.

Then I was introduced: "Oh, Your Majesty, you will know Richard Goddard…"

I could see a look of surprise flit across The Queen's face so I thought I had better help her out. I said, "Oh, Ma'am, you may remember that you opened the Henley Royal Regatta Headquarters here in Henley some twelve years ago and I was, and I still am, the Regatta Secretary."

The Queen replied, a little hesitantly…

WHAT THE QUEEN SAID TO ME:

"Umm… The Regatta Headquarters?"

The Queen had a look of vague recollection but she looked as though she needed a little more information so I replied, "Yes. It is just across the river. You went on the launch and had a boat trip that day, too."

Spiritedly, and quite clearly recollecting the previous visit, she piped up.

"Oh, yes. I remember."

Changing tack momentarily, The Queen spoke of today's boat trip, saying:

"Today, on our boat trip here, it was really quite exciting because the river was very high. It almost looked like we wouldn't get through the bridge!"

She brought the conversation back to the regatta.

"So, how are the Regatta Headquarters. Are they proving a success?"

I answered. "Yes, Ma'am. They are, thank you. I do hope you have enjoyed the museum today."

She said:

"Yes, it was very interesting. Thank you."

She then moved on. It was a lovely exchange for me but, of course, it was over so quickly.

John Redmond, Harbour Master 1991–2002 had kittens because the river was so high on that day. He was debating right to the last minute whether the trip on the launch could go ahead or not. Everyone wanted The Queen to do the trip by river but it really was touch and go.

Henley Royal Regatta has never had Queen Elizabeth ll as a prize giver. She had visited once back in 1947 as Princess Elizabeth, but never as The Queen.

In 2006 I was quite friendly with the Duke of Edinburgh's Private Secretary. I asked him if there was any chance we could get The Queen to come to Henley Royal Regatta to give the prizes that year. He said quite categorically that he was awfully sorry, but Her Majesty would be too busy. I was terribly disappointed. He did say though, that he would try and get an audience for a representative of Henley Royal Regatta at Buckingham Palace. Great news but we would have to think of a reason why The Queen would grant us that privilege.

I proceeded to tell him that Imperial College London were celebrating their 150th year anniversary, and they had said they wanted to give the Henley Royal Regatta a trophy for an event that didn't already have one. This was perfect.

The royal connection for Imperial College runs deep. Queen Victoria had laid the first brick and Prince Albert had opened Imperial College London. Also, Queen Elizabeth II is Patron of Henley Royal Regatta.

I explained this connection to Miles who suggested we write to The Queen's Private Secretary. We did this of course, and fortunately the answer came back in agreement. The Henley Royal Regatta would have an audience with The Queen. Fantastic!

Hector Miller was the silversmith who had made the trophy for Imperial College to award. It was agreed that Hector, Sir Richard Sykes, the Rector of Imperial College, myself and Mike Sweeney, the Chairman of the Henley Royal Regatta, would go to Buckingham Palace where The Queen would give a token handover of the trophy from Imperial College to Henley Royal Regatta. The trophy was to be called the Prince Albert Challenge Cup. Prince Albert was not only the founder of Imperial College but he was also the member of the Royal Family who had given Henley Royal Regatta its royal status. The Prince became President of the Henley Regatta in 1851 and thereafter it was known as Henley Royal Regatta.

On the day of the Audience, Richard Sykes brought the trophy to the palace, and Mike Sweeney and I drove up in Mike's car so we could bring the trophy back. The four of us met, and we waited in a wonderful drawing room.

We then had the etiquette talk by the equerry who told us, amongst other things, how to approach and leave The Queen. It was all very smooth.

It was our turn and, after the formality of being presented to Her Majesty, it suddenly became very relaxed and it was a very friendly and jolly experience. The Queen said…

WHAT THE QUEEN SAID TO ME...

"*Hello. How are the preparations for the Regatta going?*"

I replied, "Very well." And then I explained that the trophy was for a student event that had taken place for a number of years but did not yet have a trophy.

She asked us all about the trophy and we explained the connections to Imperial College and the historical connection between Prince Albert and the regatta. It was a very nice fifteen minutes during which she passed the trophy from Sir Richard Sykes from Imperial College to Mike Sweeney of the Henley Royal Regatta.

She seemed very interested in what was going on and we all spoke fondly of the trophy which she seemed to admire a great deal. Mike had mentioned that we would be taking the trophy back with us to Henley in his car, but when the meeting was drawing to an end and we were desperately trying to remember the etiquette of walking backwards a couple of paces, bowing, turning and walking towards the door, turn back, bow again etc., it suddenly dawned on all of us that no one actually had the trophy.

It was at this point that we should have left, but in five seconds we would be out of the door. We had to take the trophy somehow. At the same moment, The Queen's page who was standing by the door also realised the dilemma, but it was Mike who turned to The Queen, not quite knowing how to put what he wanted to say into words. So, nodding towards the page, Mike eventually came out with, "Err… Will your… Um… Will your… Err um – gremlin – bring the trophy out, Ma'am?"

To this, The Queen beamed. She roared with laughter, pointed at the page, and said,

"Gremlin, go and get it!"

It was incredibly funny and a great way to end our meeting. I feel very charmed and incredibly privileged. I am so glad The Queen had a sense of humour. I like to think that the page found it rather funny too!

Opposite: Richard Goddard and Mike Sweeney CBE with The Prince Albert Challenge Cup

SUM UP THE QUEEN IN ONE PARAGRAPH:

"On the first visit some thirty years ago, I found The Queen to be very professional and very focused. She showed interest in what was going on and she asked pertinent questions, really seeming to enjoy herself. On the second occasion, ten years or so later, she seemed to be a little more relaxed in her role as Queen. The third time, though initially a much more formal event, it was in her own environment and it turned out to be the most relaxed, chattiest and easiest meeting of them all."

CHAPTER 10

Richard Park

Life has been lucky for me really, in many ways. I have met The Queen and other Royals on a number of occasions. Also I have been lucky in what laughingly passes as a career – an enjoyable career I must say. Currently it finds me in Leicester Square, London, where I am Director of Broadcasting for Global. The moments I am about to share have been amongst the most special days of my life.

The first time I met Her Majesty was in 1986.

Originally from Scotland and with radio in my blood, the station I was working for at the time was Radio Clyde in Glasgow. A new studio complex for the station had just been completed and The Queen had accepted an invitation to make the official opening. I had been working away for six weeks prior to the opening, covering the World Cup football competition in Mexico – the one with the Maradona "hand of God" goal. This was at a time when Scotland had qualified for the competition too – something that has happened all too rarely recently.

In those days, of course, broadcasting from another country was an entirely different

Richard Park

kettle of fish in terms of technology. I mean, there were no mobiles, tweets, Skype, none of that. It's hard to think that all that was non-existent, but we actually still managed to get by and deliver a pretty good show from an exotic location.

In Mexico, the crew had been to places like Queretaro which is in the mountains about 450 miles from Mexico City, a very modest town back in those days. The football stadium was just outside its perimeter. There had been no testing of our equipment or facsimile machines to make sure we could get stories back home from this town. No technological breakthroughs had occurred. TV channels for instance, in order to get their pictures across The Atlantic, had to wait for a satellite moment and quickly send everything in that short pocket of time.

Doing the radio commentary of Scotland vs Germany from Queretaro and getting the broadcast back to Scotland was not easy at all. We would take days to set everything up and make sure the line was working and then we would wait again for a specific time the signal was up. Where I should sit in the grounds to make the most of the signal was another problem we faced. One time I ended up sitting in an open area in 90-degree heat getting shockingly sunburnt, just so we could get a line out! I subsequently got a nasty bug and felt rotten but that's by the by...

On the day of the opening in Clydebank I toured The Queen around the broadcast area, taking Her Majesty into the broadcast studios and we chatted. I was very pleasantly surprised that she was so au fait with the basic rules and principles of broadcasting technique. I don't know why I should have been surprised, of course. The Queen had been with her father, King George VI, when he was making his now famous wartime addresses via the radio. She asked a lot of really interesting and pertinent questions. Questions that only someone genuinely interested in, or had a knowledge of broadcasting, would ask.

I was relating all these stories to The Queen during her tour. I was telling her how and what it was like to work in these places, to be on the ground, what it was like to be involved with the nation's best footballers – some of the best known players the world had ever seen like Charlie Nicholas and Graeme Souness. Iconic players. We talked a lot.

I cannot quote The Queen specifically but Her Majesty asked many very relevant questions. For instance: how, because of the time difference, did we get a signal from places like Queretaro in Mexico back to the UK at the correct time of day? How did we gather our news content? She asked questions about how we found and presented our music. Many, many questions and observations. I did my best to answer them all adequately.

People asked me afterwards about my time with The Queen. I told everyone and anyone who would listen to me. My answer was always the same: "Goodness me! The Queen was utterly charming, totally knowledgeable. The level of conversation and of intelligence took my breath away." It was a wonderful experience.

WHERE: Windsor Castle
WHEN: 1999
WHY: An event called "An Evening for the Media"

In 1999, The Queen and the Duke of Edinburgh held an "Evening for the Media" at Windsor Castle and I found myself in Windsor mingling with many of the 90's megastars such as Gary Barlow, Mick Hucknall to name but a few, as Programme Director of Capital Radio.

That evening The Queen was with her Mother, Queen Elizabeth the Queen Mother and her sister, Princess Margaret. The Duke was wandering around the room meeting and greeting as he does, but I stood with The Queen, The Queen Mother and the Princess. We all chatted away and we got into a conversation about Windsor Castle.

WHAT THE QUEEN SAID TO ME...

*"I have a favourite room in the castle, you know.
Would you like me to show it to you? It is just around the corner."*

The Queen led me, with a number of other people, I hasten to add, to this room. We all walked in and, if my memory serves me correctly, it was named the "George III Dining Room".

Beaming, The Queen said:

"This is my favourite room in the castle."

And it was a most magnificent, stunning room! I could clearly see why she liked it. When we returned to the reception, Prince Philip joined us. After I was introduced, we spoke for a bit. I thought it appropriate to tell him I was just about to run a big charity event with his son, Prince Charles.

In his brusque, deep voice came the response:

*"**W**hat? What event?*
What are you talking about?"

A little perturbed, I continued quickly. "The Prince's Trust, Prince Charles' charity. It is in Hyde Park, in London. Week after next. A big music event."

Still not seeming to know what I was talking about and, more brusquely than before, the Duke snapped:

*"**W**hat? It's not the pop music is it?"*

SUM UP THE QUEEN IN ONE PARAGRAPH:

*"**T**o meet anyone in any walk of life, I am sure The Queen would be welcoming. She has an outstanding ability, with a fantastic brain and a great sense of loyalty and duty. That she wants to get out and meet as many people as she possibly can, makes her remarkable. I think she is one of this earth's most outstanding people and my admiration for her goes ocean deep, ocean deep. Like I said at the beginning of this piece, these were some of the most special days of my life. To have had the dialogues we had is very special."*

CHAPTER 11

John Gosby MBE

WHO: John Gosby MBE
WHERE: Buckingham Palace
WHEN: 8 November 1994
WHY: MBE awarded for services as a Retained Firefighter in today's Fire & Rescue Service

Totally out of the blue, I had a letter arrive in the post on Saturday, 5 May 1994. I did a double take because on the envelope was written: "On Her Majesty's Service" and "Prime Minister". I was flabbergasted! What on earth could it be? Was I really in that much trouble? Luckily I wasn't in trouble at all. In fact, it was a letter saying I had been nominated for an MBE by the Chief Fire Officer and I would be contacted in due course if my name were to appear on The Queen's Birthday Honours list.

I was invited to Buckingham Palace on 8 November, which seemed such a long time after that life-changing day back in May when I had received the first letter. I just couldn't believe this was happening. It was amazing.

Eventually the 8 November arrived. The fire service laid on a limousine and my wife, myself, my son and daughter proceeded to London and drove straight into the Buckingham Palace courtyard. The recipients – all 133 of us – were instructed on the etiquette and given a run-down on how things would progress. This was it.

John Gosby MBE

WHAT THE QUEEN SAID TO ME...

"How long have you been in the fire service?"

I answered, "Thirty-four years, Ma'am."

She then asked:

"Have you served all those years in Henley?"

To which I replied, "Nearly all, but I did do a few years in Reading."

She came back with:

"Oh yes, and do you or did you row?"

To which I replied: "Yes, I was in the Henley Rowing Club."

She then went on to say:

"Oh. I have been to the Regatta many, many years ago. I thoroughly enjoyed it and Henley is such a lovely place."

"Thank you," I said.

SUM THE QUEEN UP IN ONE PARAGRAPH:

"She looks and behaves very genuinely. She never made me feel at all inadequate; like an equal. I know she is inaccessible but she has a very good knack of making you feel relaxed and special. One other thing that impressed me was that she looks you in the eye when she speaks to you."

John Gosby MBE in uniform proudly showing off his medal

CHAPTER 12

Adam Rodgers

WHO:	Adam Rodgers
WHERE:	Bangkok, Thailand
WHEN:	28 October – 1 November 1996
WHY:	Queen's visit to Thailand

Told by Adam's Mother Jane:

As a youngster Adam lived in Thailand and twenty years ago, when this event happened he was just seven years old.

We were fortunate that Adam attended one of the few British Curriculum Schools around in those days. The school was called the Bangkok Patana School. Today it is still considered one of the most highly regarded British International schools of the many now in Bangkok.

The Queen had visited the King of Thailand – the late King Bhumibol Adulyadej and Queen Sirikit – only once before. That first visit took place in 1972. The second and last visit took place in 1996 when The Queen and Prince Phillip visited The Thai Royals again for the opening of new British Council Offices in Bangkok. A number of schoolchildren had been invited to attend one of the celebrations, which took place in the grounds of the Embassy, including Adam and his friend. The two boys were

Adam Rodgers

tasked with holding the Union flag, stretched out in front of the barrier, so that that British Royals could see it and feel welcome. They proudly held a corner each and for seven year olds it was quite a big flag. They waited patiently and then they saw her. The Queen had noticed the flag and made her way over.

She said to the two children...

WHAT THE QUEEN SAID TO ME...

"That's lovely of you to do this boys..."

The Queen was smiling. Then, with a slightly lower voice, added:

"You are holding your flag upside down though!!"

I think The Queen saw the funny side and the boys quickly corrected it but it was a memorable moment and rather amusing at the time.

The Queen with children in Thailand. This flag is not the culprit! (A Rodgers)

CHAPTER 13
Gillian Chappell

WHO: Gillian Chappell, District Commissioner of Henley District
Girl Guides, 1997–2005

WHERE: Henley-on-Thames

WHEN: 6 November 1998

WHY: Opening of Perpetual Park

I was invited to the Opening of Perpetual Park, Henley-on-Thames. The year was 1998. On this particular autumn day, there were a number of events happening throughout Henley: the opening of the River & Rowing Museum, the opening of the Henley Youth Centre and the official opening of the new Invesco Perpetual offices. I was fortunate enough to be invited to the latter in the capacity of District Commissioner of the Henley Girl Guides – so, good news! I received an invite and I was over the moon.

Allan Follett was the Mayor of Henley at the time and he helped co-ordinate the guests.

I have to say that, at this point, there had never been any talk of me actually meeting Her Majesty. So, to my utter surprise, totally out of the blue and only the night prior to the visit, Allan rang me and said, "I've got a favour to ask you. I need to get a group of people together in a line up to meet The Queen and I would very much like

Gillian Chappell

to ask you if you would join that line up." He added, tongue-in-cheek, that it would also bring down the average age of the group considerably if I accepted. In hindsight I was quite pleased I didn't have too much time to worry about it. So the day came and I took my position.

In any line up, The Queen doesn't always speak to everyone. She wouldn't have enough time. On this occasion, I was a little unfortunate to be standing next to a lady who The Queen had a long conversation with. It just happened that this lady had taught The Queen to drive when she had been in the Auxiliary Territorial Service (ATS). They were reminiscing over those bygone days back in 1945. I don't know if The Queen was briefed or not but they had this long conversation about how much The Queen loves driving and how "they" were trying to stop her.

It was a hard act to follow. After such a nice conversation with that particular lady, The Queen moved on to me. She recognised the uniform straightaway. Her Majesty Queen Elizabeth had been Patron of Girlguiding, and Queen Elizabeth the Queen Mother had been a District Commissioner in the very early days of Girlguiding. In fact, a Brownies pack had been set up at Buckingham Palace for Queen Elizabeth and her sister, Princess Margaret, to attend. It was called the 1st Buckingham Palace unit. So really there is a very strong Royal Family link with Girlguiding.

So, The Queen having recognised the uniform, looked at me and she asked…

WHAT THE QUEEN SAID TO ME...

"*So how is the guiding going in Henley?*"

I replied with, "It's thriving. It really is going incredibly well. We are very lucky." I then decided to add, "But we struggle to get the leaders."

The Queen, clearly concerned about the time schedule, was just at the point of moving on to the next person, when she gave me a sideways look, smiled and said:

"That's what they all say!"

It was rather amusing.

SUM THE QUEEN UP IN ONE PARAGRAPH:

"Very professional. She knew what her job in Henley was and she did it really well."

CHAPTER 14

Allan Follett

WHO:	Allan Follett, Mayor of Henley-on-Thames from 1998–1999
WHERE:	River & Rowing Museum, Henley-on-Thames
WHEN:	Late autumn 1998
WHY:	Grand Opening of the museum

It also happened to be the opening of the new Invesco Perpetual offices which were built just behind the River & Rowing Museum, but my involvement on this particular day was for the grand opening of the River & Rowing Museum. As Mayor, I was involved in the organisation of the event along with the Henley-on-Thames Town Council as they owned the land where the museum is situated.

The plan involved The Queen arriving by boat to a temporary jetty outside the museum. However, rivers are unpredictable and the Thames was behaving in a rather contrary way in the lead up to the event. It was all rather touch and go. However, the big question was: if The Queen was going to arrive by boat, where was she going to embark?

The obvious thought was to use the land where the Henley Royal Regatta takes place, but that land is in Berkshire! This went against strict protocol as The Queen is always greeted by the Lord Lieutenant of the county she is visiting, so landing in Berkshire would have caused a massive headache! Sir Hugo Brunner, the Lord

Allan Follett

Lieutenant of Oxfordshire, was scheduled to meet her, not the Lord Lieutenant of Berkshire so it was decided that Phyllis Court on the Oxfordshire bank of the River Thames was to be the place of embarkation.

A special jetty had been built at the River & Rowing Museum in the hope that it would be used for *Windrush*, the Royal Barge, to land and moor up to. I recall the river was running quite fast that day and it was still touch and go as to whether the boat would make the trip. However, the decision was made and it was decided that *Windrush* was more than capable of the job. It brought The Queen safely under the Henley Bridge and upstream to the museum.

My duties started when *Windrush* arrived. I was to meet Her Majesty from the jetty, greet her and then introduce her to a number of people involved with the museum, the Royal British Legion and the Henley Wildlife Group.

When telling Her Majesty that I was going to introduce her to the latter she seemed quite amused. I think I must have emphasised the word *wildlife* a little more than I should have, as she looked at me with a sideways glance and said...

WHAT THE QUEEN SAID TO ME...

"Oooh 'wildlife'!"

It was as if I had meant big cats or something! I refrained from saying so.

I then escorted her though the crowds of children that had gathered all along the river – all very happy and waving flags, really getting into the swing of things. About halfway along, she turned to me, looked me in the eyes and said…

"You have an awful lot of children, don't you?"

I said, "Yes Ma'am." I stopped myself, but I was so close to saying, "Well, they are not all mine, Ma'am!" but I didn't. I managed to hold back and I'm glad I did, certainly at the time anyway. I still wonder to this day, however, what she would have said if I had actually blurted that line out.

After a break for me, and after The Queen was escorted around the museum, lunch was served. I was given the responsibility and the pleasure of proposing the Royal toast which was a massive privilege, particularly as it is not often that the toast is done when The Queen is actually present.

At the end of the visit she did say, "Thank you very much. It's been lovely meeting all the different people from Henley."

SUM THE QUEEN UP IN ONE PARAGRAPH:

"Genuinely interested in what all of the people she met were saying to her. A very gracious lady, very calm and she made it a very easy day for me."

CHAPTER 15
Janet Leaver

WHO: Janet Leaver, Chairman Henley WI
WHERE: Henley-on-Thames
WHEN: 1998
WHY: Opening of Perpetual Park

I was asked if I would like to be presented to The Queen on her visit to Henley for the Royal Opening of Perpetual Park.

Allan Follett, Mayor of Henley at the time, had put together a list of local people who were running other things in the town. I was Chairman of Henley Women's Institute (WI) Markets. This later became known as the Country Markets.

The WI had been producing goods to sell at these markets every Friday for years. We sold good, locally produced products and I had a wonderful time being the chair. Unfortunately, we closed the country markets about five years ago which was a rather sad time for me.

When Allan approached me, I immediately said yes. He told me I would be able to bring a friend so I took a lady who was also a market producer. On the day we actually had some really nice weather. In the lead up to the event we had had so much rain, I think we were all rather worried, but luckily the day itself was lovely.

Janet Leaver

Invesco Perpetual put on a great show that day. They really went to town and we, the WI, were asked to make some cakes.

Between all the ladies we made fifteen hundred pieces of cake for this event! Fifteen hundred! There were five hundred proper butterfly cakes, five hundred cookies and five hundred pieces of shortbread. All were displayed in great big glass jars with big fancy tops on, which stood about a metre high on the tables.

Our lovely WI members had done a great job and they did look nice all presented there in prime position. I don't actually know what happened to them or, in fact, if the cakes and cookies ever got eaten! I like to think they were given to a charity after the event and they were eaten, but I really don't know what became of them.

I stood in the line up next to a very tall couple who I didn't know. The Queen came along the line, and Allan introduced Her Majesty to me saying, "This is Janet Leaver. She is Chairman of the WI Markets."

WHAT THE QUEEN SAID TO ME...

"Have you had a market today?"

It was a Friday and we had never missed a market so I replied, "Yes, we have. But we didn't have a lot of customers this morning. I think they were all down by the river waiting for you, Your Majesty."

She said with a look of concern:

"Oh! Well, that's very nice if they were, but I'm sure they all have very muddy shoes. It was rather muddy down there from what I could see."

I smiled and then that was it. I said, "Yes" and "Thank you" and The Queen moved on.

SUM THE QUEEN UP IN ONE PARAGRAPH:

"The Queen made the conversation and she made me feel very relaxed. It became very easy but it was over too quickly. When you shake her hand it is not really a shake but more of a little tiny touch. She is a very sweet lady."

"I did actually go to a garden party for the WI only a fortnight ago at Buckingham Palace but it was Camilla, The Duchess of Cornwall, not The Queen who was hosting the party. We were approached by a lovely tall man who asked my friend and I if we wanted to be presented to Sophie, Countess of Wessex. The Countess asked us about the WI and was very natural, lovely and easy to talk to. She told us she belongs to the Bagshot WI. Birgitte, Duchess of Gloucester, was there too and she was happily chatting away to people. It was a wonderful day, all china tea sets and, I have to say, the bathrooms were amazing. I was exhausted and shattered by the end of the day though."

CHAPTER 16

Jean Pickett

WHO: Jean Pickett, Town Clerk (historic title for Chief Executive), Henley-on-Thames Town Council

WHERE: River & Rowing Museum, Henley-on-Thames

WHEN: 6 November 1998

WHY: Dedication/Official Opening of the River & Rowing Museum

As Town Clerk I assisted with the civic arrangements for The Queen's visit to Henley-on-Thames in 1998 for the purpose of officially opening the River & Rowing Museum. The museum actually opened to the public in August 1998 but this event happened in November 1998. It was nice because my grandchildren were some of the first children to visit the museum and their names appear in the visitors' book alongside others including our local celebrity, Phillip Schofield.

The museum sits on council land on a ninety-nine year lease. Historically the annual payment is a rose given to the town council, which I believe still happens to this day; it certainly did when I held the position.

When the Town Council was notified that The Queen would open the museum, the civic arrangements started. There was a lot of work to do. There were numerous meetings with the police and security services. We had discussions with divers who

Jean Pickett

would check the River Thames, and several meetings with the police guards. We had many talks with Phyllis Court in Henley, where Her Majesty would embark on the Royal Barge, *Windrush*. There were also lots of discussions with the Environment Agency who supplied the launch. One really amazing thing that struck me at the time was how nobody knew everything.

We designated a special loo for Her Majesty and a secure phone line for her to use if necessary. It was all quite daunting and, of course, I had a sudden panic of the female kind; the kind of panic that fills many a woman with dread. What was I going to wear for such an important occasion? After a large amount of painful deliberation, I chose a rather nice red and black dress. The Queen also wore red! Good decision I thought.

One thing, of course, we could not predict was the weather. Luckily the day came and it turned out beautifully; the sun was out and it was really a rather splendid day.

I was in the line up and ready to be introduced, standing among the good and important people of the town, dignitaries and common folk. Then my turn came. Hugo Brunner introduced me. "This is Jean Pickett. She has the title of Town Clerk," and The Queen said…

WHAT THE QUEEN SAID TO ME…

"That is a historic title!"

I replied, "Yes, Ma'am. With the added honour of being the first female town clerk in the town's history."

"Well done. And this occasion has clearly been well organised."

I said, "Thank you, Ma'am," thinking that was going to be it.

But then The Queen asked, turning to my husband,

"And you, Sir, are the important support behind the scenes?"

My husband, smiling, replied, "I certainly hope so, Ma'am. It is much needed sometimes."

She responded with,

"And appreciated, no doubt. The weather is very kind to us today considering the time of year."

I then replied, "Yes, Ma'am. It is quite a relief and thank you for your visit today."

SUM THE QUEEN UP IN ONE PARAGRAPH:

"She involves people. She doesn't ignore anyone and she has the most porcelain skin. She is petite, extremely smart and comes across as a very intelligent lady."

CHAPTER 17

Bill Mundy

WHO:	Bill Mundy
WHERE:	Henley-on-Thames
WHEN:	1998
WHY:	Perpetual Park official opening

A little preamble to this story by the author:

A renowned artist, Bill Mundy is well known throughout the world for his miniature portraits. His reputation precedes him, having won every miniature competition worldwide at some point and being the only living artist to have a miniature portrait painting permanently exhibited in the Victoria and Albert Museum in London.

Bill also exhibits at the Royal Academy – the first painting he had hung there was in 1977 and was a portrait of the Sultan of Johor. Bill's paintings were voted "exhibit of the year" at The Royal Academy's Summer Exhibition in both 1980 and 1982.

Bill also paints using other techniques including large oil portraits, however, and only in my opinion, Bill's *trompe l'oeil* paintings are the most incredible. Translated to "deceive the eye" *trompe l'oeil* paintings require meticulous attention to detail and an enhanced understanding of perspective. Every minute detail is observed. Accuracy of size (each item painted will be the exact same size as the original) and accuracy of colour, light and shadow are all imperative to the success of each painting. The end product has to be an exact replica of the original.

Bill Mundy

Bill Mundy's Painting of Phantom Gold that was given as a gift to The Queen

It has been an incredible journey thus far for Bill. As part of that journey he has written a number of books on miniature portrait painting and has also published his fascinating autobiography entitled *A Brush with Life*.

This is Bill's brush with Royalty:

Back in 1997, the wife of a local businessman commissioned me to paint a large oil painting of her husband. The subject, Sir Martyn Arbib, was the founder of a company called Perpetual and in 1998 Perpetual's new offices in Henley-on-Thames were being officially opened by Her Majesty The Queen.

After the oil was completed Martyn commissioned me to paint a number of miniature portraits of his family and as a direct result of the success of these commissions he asked me if I would consider painting something suitable for him to give as a gift to The Queen on the day of the opening. I was thrilled to be asked and we discussed what that painting might be of. It needed to be relevant yet original.

At the time Martyn had a keen interest in race horses. We all know The Queen shares this interest so Martyn suggested it might be a nice idea to have a miniature made of The Queen's horse, Phantom Gold, winning the Perpetual Stakes at Newbury in October 1995. I was happy with his suggestion and the decision was made.

Martyn kindly supplied me with a photograph of Phantom Gold and I sketched up a rough. This was sent to Buckingham Palace for approval which duly came. The final painting was approximately five inches by four inches. It was set within a gold plated, oval frame and included the name of the horse, the event and the date. We were both very happy with the end product.

I had been invited to attend the opening and was awaiting The Queen's arrival with Sir Martyn, the painting and a number of other guests. The Queen arrived and Martyn presented the miniature to her. He then turned and introduced me. I approached The Queen just as she came forward and we started to chat. We spoke for a while. The conversation was mainly about the painting and of my art.

WHAT THE QUEEN SAID TO ME...

"Do you specialise in painting horses?"

I said: "No, apart from in my early days when I was a lithographic designer and occasionally painted horses for decoration on biscuit tins, these days I specialise in portraiture."

The Queen asked:

"Oh. Who have you painted?"

I smiled and told her, "Well actually I have painted Prince Phillip at Buckingham Palace. I was commissioned to paint his portrait by The Game Conservancy. As you probably know, he is their Patron."

The Queen smiled at the mention of her husband and we continued chatting about some of the other people I have painted. I explained that when I lived in Singapore I painted many members of the Malay Royal Family and since then have painted hundreds of portraits. The Queen did tell me that she liked the painting of Phantom Gold very much. It was very nice to hear.

Throughout the conversation The Queen appeared genuinely interested. She finished with: "How interesting" and my time was over.

SUM UP THE QUEEN IN ONE PARAGRAPH:

"The Queen has a flawless complexion. A sparkle, a twinkle in her eyes that's for sure. She also has a great sense of humour. Yes, she was really quite chatty, surprisingly so considering how many people there were around that day. Although I was naturally at ease, Her Majesty does have a knack of making one feel very comfortable. What a genuinely nice and happy woman she is."

A Bill Mundy painting of Prince Phillip

CHAPTER 18

Sir John Madejski OBE, DL, DLITT

WHO:	Sir John Madejski OBE, DL, DLITT
WHERE:	Buckingham Palace and Sandringham
WHEN:	2000, 2006
WHY:	OBE awarded for services to Reading

Strangely, I was not at all nervous!

My mother was in the audience which was lovely for me and, I know, a very proud moment for her. Unfortunately, and very sadly, by the time I got my knighthood in 2009, which was awarded by Princess Anne, my mother had passed away. I know she would have been incredibly proud.

My OBE was for services to Reading. My largesse was well known in Reading town and the surrounding areas, but – contrary to popular belief – it was not all football-related. In London, I have also been a benefactor to the Royal Academy of Art and to the Victoria & Albert Museum, but this was not what the OBE was for.

In the lead up to the investiture, a courtier meets all the recipients in an ante-chamber and gives everyone a quick reminder on the protocol. Kind but firm, and everything is done with impeccable precision. When the courtier had finished his briefing, he asked if there were any questions. I thought this was a good time to bring up something that

Sir John Madejski

had been worrying me. People had been getting the pronunciation of my name wrong all my life, and I really didn't want that to happen today.

I said to him, "Actually, I have quite an unusual name – it's John Ma-day-ski," making sure I pronounced it clearly for him.

He replied, very reassuringly, with "Oh don't worry, old chap, they know everything." I was put at ease and I confidently snaked up a line of probably one hundred people to receive my honour. My turn arrived and I was ready to go when – to my utter horror – I heard the announcer pipe up and say, "John Mad-jew-ski." I could have flipping well throttled him!

WHAT THE QUEEN SAID TO ME...

"Congratulations. I hear you have done some remarkable work with Reading."

I nodded and said, "Yes. Thank you."

I shook her hand lightly, and suddenly drew a blank. I don't know why. Possibly because of the Mad-jew-ski moment, memory of all protocol went out of my mind, and I suddenly found myself turning around to walk away!

We had been told to back away from The Queen, facing her at all times and to never turn our back. I couldn't believe it. "Arrgh" was going on in my head, and I very much hoped that maybe she hadn't noticed!

On my moment of realisation, which was probably only a second – probably only half a second – I quickly turned back to face her. I hoped I did it with the least amount of disruption. Nothing was said. Not a comment was made. I think I got away with it. Phew! I laugh in hindsight but at the time I was mortified.

When it came to me getting my knighthood, I made absolutely sure that, firstly, I would not make the same mistake again and, secondly, they would get my name right. Thankfully, they did and when the Leader of Ceremonies announced me, he said, "Sir John Ma-day-ski," I was so pleased. The Princess Royal gave me this one. I backed away as I should have done the first time, and no mistakes were made on either part – thank goodness.

WHERE: Sandringham Military Academy

WHEN: 12 April 2006

WHY: The Sovereign's Parade

A friend of mine, Major-General Andrew Ritchie CBE, was Commandant at Sandhurst Military Academy at the time. His wife, Camilla, invited me to The Sovereign's Parade at Sandhurst to which I was delighted to accept. It is a big event at the end of each term that marks the passing out of young commissioned officers after an awful lot of hard work. It is a very big and proud day for all the families there.

The day of the parade came and I turned up with my daughter, Camilla, where we met Andrew and Camilla at their lovely house on the Sandhurst Estate. We were ushered in, and were relaxing with mutual friends when suddenly I realised we were actually in a sitting room filled with many members of the Royal Family!

When the initial surprise passed we relaxed a little and the day continued. We all went to watch the parade.

A wonderful sight of officer cadets who had just completed the commissioning course, brilliantly marching past in perfect formation. This was such an inspirational sight and a delight to watch. When the parade had finished we moved to The Great Hall, I think it was called, where parents, guests and the newly passed out officer cadets were gathered.

The Queen and Sir Andrew started working the room. They were meeting all the parents and families of the newly appointed officers. This particular day was extra special for The Queen because Prince Harry had also just "passed out". Sir Andrew had escorted Her Majesty and completed half of the room when – out of the blue and totally unexpectedly – he brought The Queen up and introduced her to Camilla, my daughter, and myself. He then proceeded to say, "Oh, John, would you mind very much looking after Her Majesty for a minute or two? There is something I really must do straightaway."

I was gobsmacked! There I was standing with my daughter and The Queen of England. Mindboggling! We could also see she was feeling a tad uncomfortable at this slight alteration to her agenda. Camilla and I were dumbfounded and feeling slightly awkward. Not knowing quite what to say and feeling rather put on the spot, I decided to say, "Oh, Ma'am, you must be so delighted about your Grandson being made an officer today." And she said…

WHAT THE QUEEN SAID TO ME:

"*Oh, yes. It's... um... Yes, lovely.*"

She was clearly very bemused at having to speak to us in this kind of awkward situation. She did utter a few things that, due to me being rather overwhelmed, I didn't quite understand, but we chugged on through.

SUM THE QUEEN UP IN ONE PARAGRAPH:

"*I have both a profound sympathy and an admiration for her. Everywhere she goes she is introduced to people – hundreds of people – who, of course, are overwhelmed by the experience and she just keeps on doing it. It is such a thrill to meet The Queen and I can't praise her enough. She is stoic, regal, warm, gracious, faultless, magnanimous and hardworking. I believe she has been the perfect Queen. Even on the Royal Barge, on the Thames, for The Queen's Jubilee, she didn't venture below. It was a cold day but she knew people were on the banks to see her and she stayed on deck. Hats off to her! I am delighted I've been able to meet her.*"

CHAPTER 19

Tony Hobbs MBE

WHO: Tony Hobbs MBE, Royal Waterman to Her Majesty The Queen, 1981-2001

WHERE: Buckingham Palace

WHEN: 2002

WHY: Royal Watermen get-together, as part of The Queen's Golden Jubilee celebrations

The Company of Watermen is a tradition going back to the year 1514; in fact, last year was the 500th anniversary. The Queen's Watermen, or Royal Watermen, is a tradition going back some 800 years with the watermen having rowed King John to Runnymede for the signing of the Magna Carta back in 1215. The 500th and 800th anniversaries were jointly celebrated in 2014, celebrations in which I was part and celebrations I will tell you about later, but for now I would prefer to start the story at the beginning.

You see, 500 years ago the River Thames in London was alive with boats and ferries and barges and business houses. This was ultimately because transportation by river was the easiest and quickest way. If you could afford to have a barge, it was quicker to be rowed on the river than to navigate through the narrow and filthy streets of London. The Royal Watermen were started in order to row the monarch either on state occasions or from palace to palace – Greenwich, Westminster, Hampton Court and the Tower of London. The transportation of the monarch was the watermen's sole purpose back then; these days their responsibilities are purely ceremonial.

Tony Hobbs MBE

Though we are called "watermen" there are times – increasingly so, in fact – that we don't actually go out on the water and, on these occasions, the watermen sit on the back of the Royal Carriage as "boxmen" in their wonderful Elizabethan uniforms. This type of transportation is used now for the State Opening of Parliament when The Queen's processions would go to the Palace of Westminster.

To date there are twenty-four of us still retained by the monarch under the control of the Queen's Bargemaster, and any appointments would take place on the Thames in London. There have been a few exceptions to that rule over the decades, in that the Royal Watermen have gone elsewhere. Henley-on-Thames is one example. Though still on the River Thames, it is some way out of London.

I was aboard as a waterman for both the River and Rowing Museum and the Henley Royal Regatta Headquarters openings. It was a rare event and certainly very special for me to be afloat in my uniform and to be in my home town not just once but twice; two very proud moments for me. I would say I was in The Queen's company at least forty or fifty times over two decades and in all the years I did duties as a Royal Waterman I spoke to The Queen only once. Ironically, that was ashore.

The occasion was The Queen's Golden Jubilee celebrations of 2002. All of the serving and retired Royal Watermen and their wives were invited to Buckingham Palace to celebrate. During the reception, The Queen spent an incredibly long time with all of us. I am sure that Her Majesty spoke to every single person that day.

That was when I had my one and only conversation with The Queen. It was most certainly worth the wait and the experience was incredible.

My wife and I were introduced as "Mr and Mrs Hobbs from Henley-on-Thames".

Tony Hobbs MBE in full Waterman Uniform. Painting by Bill Mundy.

WHAT THE QUEEN SAID TO ME...

"*Oh yes, Henley.*"

I can't be sure, but she looked like she was recollecting her two previous visits, so I said, "Yes. We had the honour of transporting you four years ago when you opened the River and Rowing Museum." I added, "You came aboard the Royal Barge, *Windrush*, at the Phyllis Court Club and we took you through the Henley bridge upriver to the opening of the River and Rowing Museum."

"Oh, yes!" she exclaimed. "Through the Henley bridge. I remember. Just! We only just got through though, didn't we!"

On the day in question, the River Thames was in flood. It was a wonderfully bright November day but we had had heavy rain in the lead-up. It was debatable right to the last moment whether we were in fact going to pick Her Majesty up at Phyllis Court and bring her by boat through the bridge to the museum or seek an alternative plan. It was clearly a memorable day for her, and I was absolutely amazed at Her Majesty's memory. After carrying out hundreds of duties and meeting hundreds of people in those previous four years, The Queen remembered that one particular day when the river was so high it nearly jeopardised her river trip. Wonderful!

Watermen on land and opposite on the water. Tony 4th in red from left on board 'Windrush'

SUM THE QUEEN UP IN ONE PARAGRAPH:

"She is a fantastic woman. She could have retired many years ago and had a relaxing retirement walking around the gardens with her corgis, but she has kept going. The stamina that lady must have is just incredible – and the Duke of Edinburgh too – for people of that age. I mean, I am no spring chicken and I get tired rather quickly. The Queen stands for ages; like, at the Cenotaph she stands so still and sometimes she is on her feet for hours. I think she is really just marvellous."

Charles Burns

WHO: Charles Burns, silhouette artist
WHERE: Ritz Hotel, London and St James' Palace
WHEN: 2002, 2006, 2011
WHY: I am an entertainer

STORY NO. 1

Many people think that silhouette-cutting is a long and complicated process – photographs, shadows, drawing, tracing and so on. It is not. When I cut a silhouette, I pull my scissors from my trousers, poise the black paper in my hand and cut freehand on the spot. Behind the black paper there is a white piece and this is used as a negative. The cut takes all of a minute to do. I then mount the portrait on a little card and give it to the guest at the party.

It is a very traditional English art and silhouette artists are a rare breed. I am a huge fan of Hubert Leslie who cut silhouettes on Brighton Pier in the 1920s and 1930s. It was largely by studying his duplicate albums now housed in the National Portrait Gallery that I taught myself to cut silhouettes. I have over 150,000 silhouettes in my duplicate album and the collection is still growing.

The first time I actually got to meet The Queen was in 2002 at a party for about 250 guests at The Ritz Hotel to celebrate the Golden Jubilee. It soon became apparent this

Charles Burns

event was going to be much more relaxed than normal and that The Queen was there to enjoy herself. The Queen had been informed that she would meet a magician that day and that she would also have her silhouette cut. I had also been informed that I would cut her that day, so we both knew I was there to do a job.

It was a strange event for me. I knew I was working and knew I had to cut the silhouette of The Queen, but how was I supposed to make that silhouette happen? How on earth does one approach The Queen?

About halfway through the evening I thought I would make my move. I manoeuvred myself and waited until the person talking to The Queen at the time was just about to finish and, well, I just walked up to her, smiled and said, "Good evening, Your Majesty" and "Good evening, Sir," to the chap The Queen was just about to finish talking to. "Hi. I hope you don't mind me joining you. I'm Charles Burns, the silhouette artist. I will be doing some silhouettes of you and your guests tonight. I wondered if you would like to have one done now."

The silhouette of The Queen and Prince Phillip cut by Charles Burns

WHAT THE QUEEN SAID TO ME...

"*Oh yes, okay.*"

She was smiling. I told her she had to be standing sideways on to me, so she turned to face the chap who then said, "Oh, Your Majesty. You could have it for your next stamp!" I know my hands were shaking and I wasn't one hundred per cent pleased with my effort, but The Queen did go off around the room holding her silhouette.

STORY NO. 2

The second time I met The Queen was also at The Ritz, in 2006. The occasion was The Queen's 80th Birthday.

Now, apparently The Queen doesn't like surprises, she likes to know who will be at an event and what will happen. I was minding my own business when I suddenly felt a tap on the shoulder. A voice said: "Her Majesty will have her silhouette done now."

I was led to where The Queen was and I introduced myself again. "Good evening, Your Majesty. I am Charles Burns." The Queen looked at me and said...

WHAT THE QUEEN SAID TO ME...

"*I rather think you have done me before.*"

I said, "Yes. I do hope I can do a little better this time! Would you like a silhouette done in full length?"

Smiling, she said...

"No. No. Just the bust will be fine."

and we both laughed...

STORY NO. 3

My last meeting with The Queen was in 2011 at a party in St James' Palace, organised and hosted by Lady Elizabeth Anson. Lady Elizabeth did the introductions.

Addressing The Queen directly, she said, "Oh, you know Charles. He cut your silhouette at your 80th birthday party."

WHAT THE QUEEN SAID TO ME...

"Oh yes. I do remember."

Lady Elizabeth went on to ask if The Queen would like another one cut, saying she knew I had my scissors here.

"No. Once is enough, but I do remember you doing it."

I told The Queen I was flattered that she should remember such a thing. She gave me a rather withering look and said,

"Well, of course I remember – it's in my bedroom!"

Wow! Fantastic! In her bedroom!! The Queen's bedroom! What more can you ask of your work?

SUM UP THE QUEEN IN ONE PARAGRAPH:

> "*At the Queen's Birthday Party, a fellow entertainer pointed something out to me. He said that, although the event was deliberately informal, and The Queen was mingling as any other guest, it was always obvious where The Queen was among the five hundred or so guests, despite her diminutive form. It was as if an unseen spotlight was always shining on her. This is my most abiding impression of her.*"

> "*My silhouttes were published in the Diamond Jubilee souvenir edition of 'Hello!' Magazine in June 2012. It was to be an exclusive. I was so, so proud, and I feel a lot less reticent now talking about my meetings with The Queen.*"

CHAPTER 21

Timothy Haigh MBE

WHO: Timothy Haigh MBE
WHERE: Buckingham Palace
WHEN: 2003
WHY: Investiture. Receiving MBE for services to education

From an early age my parents instilled in me a belief in the power of education. When I was young, education was very black and white: if you passed the 11+ you were more likely to have a successful future career and if you failed, life was more likely to be something of a struggle. I had two goes at the 11+ and failed twice. Consequently, I went to the local secondary modern; a tough place to be in those days and I did not enjoy it. All in all I had a pretty hard time.

Though it was never discussed I'm sure my father knew it was not easy for me. One night he came home from work and said we were going on our bikes to meet someone. In a bedsit on the other side of town lived a teacher from a well known local Public school. To make ends meet, this teacher did private tutoring in his spare time and that is why we were there. For the first time in my life a teacher had time to explain things to me and as a result of this extra help I passed the 13+, a huge turning point in my life.

I can honestly say that we would not be sitting here in Henley today if my father hadn't taken me on that cycle ride on a cold and dark autumn evening to meet that tutor.

Timothy Haigh MBE

Another major step in my personal development was when my father took me into town and introduced me to the youth centre. It was a place where I met new people and new challenges. It opened my eyes to the many opportunities life had, including sailing, still a very big love of mine today.

My love of sailing and the sea led me to the Merchant Navy and, after leaving the Navy and starting my eventual career, I got married and had children.

Whilst I had young children at primary school I was asked to help at the youth centre, soon becoming the Warden/Youth Club Leader. I was very keen to expand the horizons of some of the not so well off or not so well looked after kids in the area. I wanted to be an adult that these kids could feel comfortable with, a mentor. I knew that if we could hold onto these young adults until they were eighteen or nineteen years old then generally they would go on to have a good life.

It was at the primary school that my children attended where I became a Governor. The Head was a very special lady. It was the first new-build school in the town and the first not to have desks lined up in strict rows. The Head and staff were all genuinely and enthusiastically dedicated to ensuring all children succeeded to the best of their individual abilities and all felt good about themselves. After many exciting and fulfilling years suddenly thirty years had gone by. I felt the school was in good heart and handed over to a new and enthusiastic Chair. I had great confidence they would maintain and grow the ethos of the school.

A number of years before I stepped down from the governing body, totally out of the blue, I received a letter from the Houses of Parliament. The letter informed me that The Queen was minded to present me with an MBE and would I accept. Shocked, but yes of course I would accept. It was for services to education and, I felt, a recognition for the staff, governors and all the parents who had created such a wonderful environment in which all of its children have such an excellent start to their lives.

I found out that it was the wonderful Head at the time who had nominated me but very sadly she passed away before I actually received the award. It was some consolation that she did know I was actually going to get the MBE and I hope she felt the award was also recognition for her and her staff. Her passing was very sad and hard for the school. If she were watching now, I know she would be proud that her school remains as successful as ever and retains her caring ethos.

So, in 2003, I went to Buckingham Palace with my wife and two sons. It was very exciting but I didn't feel particularly nervous. I did think about my parents. They are both deceased but I thought about how proud they would have been and what a critical moment that bike ride had been all those years ago. My father, before being a policeman, was a Grenadier Guardsman and had served at Buckingham Palace. He told a story of how Princess Elizabeth and Princess Margaret would play tag round his legs as he'd stand to attention in the gardens at the rear of the Palace.

Whatever would he have thought of my being there as a guest of her Majesty! I felt very honoured to be in this place with this group of special people and now it was my turn.

WHAT THE QUEEN SAID TO ME...

"What is your award for?"

Tim Haigh MBE with wife Jacquie and son Julian on the day of the investiture

I replied with: "I am Chair of Governors for a very successful school which I have been associated with for many years." I went on to say that we worked to balance the child's development between helping them to grow as confident young adults whilst still achieving good academic results but, most of all, ensuring they felt carefree and happy and enjoyed their time with us.

It kind of all poured out but time went so fast.

The Queen said in reply:

"That hat is wonderful and so important."

And then as quickly as that it was over.

I walked away from the Queen and backstage to the gentleman who congratulates you, unclips the medal from your lapel and places it in its box. It was all really nicely done, the whole day was such a charming experience.

Reunited with my family, we all spilled out into the yard afterwards and had photographs taken. A lot of smiles and happiness everywhere. It was all just lovely but to top it off for me, my elder son who is in the Royal Navy and was in uniform, was approached by the Admiral of the Fleet, the First Sea Lord, who had also received an award that day. He came across to shake my son's hand and speak to him. I felt very proud and thought of my father and mother and of the journey our family had made.

SUM UP THE QUEEN IN ONE PARAGRAPH:

"I found The Queen to be a warm, friendly and efficient woman."

CHAPTER 22

Melba Pitt MBE

WHO: Melba Pitt MBE

Founder of the South Oxfordshire branch of MENCAP

WHERE: Buckingham Palace

WHEN: 2003

WHY: Awarded MBE for services to disabled young people and to the community in Henley-on-Thames, Oxfordshire

I set up a toy library about fifty years ago and, about five years later, I founded the South Oxfordshire MENCAP as an offshoot of the toy library.

There had been a failed attempt a few years earlier to set it up and I thought the time was right to try again. It had become apparent to me that the parents and carers of children and adults with learning difficulties desperately needed a voice, and I guess I thought I was the person to be that voice. A meeting was arranged and MENCAP South Oxfordshire was born.

Back then we met at the clinic in Henley on the hospital campus with the idea and main aim of getting people together and meeting others that were like them. We already had specialised play equipment for those with disabilities and learning problems which was great, but it was hard. Back in those days, these people were

Melba Pitt MBE

locked away and weren't expected to mix with "normal" people. It was as if they didn't exist or they had to be kept secret. We managed to get young volunteers who would come to help. Sometimes they would play instruments or sing, but ultimately they were there to help make the lives of these people with disability issues richer and more interwoven with outside society. It took a lot of time and effort but it was worth it tenfold and I can proudly say it is still flourishing.

I retired a couple of years ago because of my eyes, but I am still a member of MENCAP. Well, actually I'm President and I'm still very interested in their work. I have always, and still do, write pantomimes for them, having had a background in singing. That's every couple of years and I love doing it. The toy library is now a sensory room but it is still going, and it is administered by Nomad, the Baptist wing at the d:two in Henley.

It was twelve years ago in 2003 when this lovely letter arrived in my letterbox totally out of the blue. It took a while to sink in when I realised what it was. Receiving a letter from 10 Downing Street is quite a thing – you wonder what on earth it could be! I had to keep quiet which was so frustrating, and I had to wait to be told when I could tell everybody. It seemed such a long wait. Mind you, I did tell my husband. I told him to sit down first though! In fact, I don't think he believed me, it was such a shock. Well, it was a great surprise. You know, when you do these sorts of things you never expect anything like this to happen; you just do them because you feel so strongly. It is never expected, which is what makes it special! After what seemed like an age I got the letter saying I could tell. I was so excited. The letter came with instructions outlining all the whats and wherefores, and I was told I could bring three guests.

My husband, daughter, her partner and I went to Buckingham Palace in a special car. Yes, you tend to feel like you really have to hire a limousine. When we pulled up at the palace, staff had a wheelchair waiting for my husband and he was very well looked after. It was like they had thought of everything.

We had a little lecture by this amazing man who was so, so funny, telling us how we should conduct ourselves: Ma'am as in jam, not Ma'am as in sparm etc. We had all these things to remember as well as the excitement of the event. I like to think I remembered them all. Well I hope so, though there is a tiny part of me that has a horrible feeling that I may not have bowed when I left Her Majesty. I was so full of what I had been talking about, you see, that I just can't remember!

When the time came to receive my MBE, I found I wasn't too nervous at all. I had performed with my singing many times in the past and that definitely helped keep the nerves away. I was called and I made my curtsey.

WHAT THE QUEEN SAID TO ME...

"This is a very specialised area that you are involved in. How did you get involved?"

I explained: "Having had four very healthy children myself, my heart went out to a neighbour who had a Down's syndrome boy. It started me thinking about other people with children with learning difficulties, and that someone really should do something about it."

I went on to tell her about those days which really weren't so long ago; about how these girls and boys, men and women were kept out of society and were not expected to mingle. Also how "normal" people had never really met people like them, and how ordinary folk didn't know people like this existed. I got to a point where I thought I should probably stop as I do get rather passionate!

Melba Pitt MBE with husband David Kingsley Pitt on the day of the investiture.
A proud couple.

She said genuinely,

*"**H**ow very interesting."*

Unfortunately, I knew my time was over. I did speak to The Queen for quite a bit longer than she spoke to me, but she made me feel so relaxed, and she really showed a genuine interest in what I was saying. She looked at me all the time. I am so proud of the fact that I have been made an MBE, but I rarely attach the letters MBE when I sign my name. On occasion I will use it and having MBE at the end of my signature does have its advantages, particularly for the charity. If you want to impress someone or to gain a little gravitas it can surely help!

SUM THE QUEEN UP IN ONE PARAGRAPH:

*"**S**he is a person I like talking to and I really feel that I would like to go on talking to her about all kinds of subjects. I do still have that feeling, even now. More to the point – and rightly or wrongly – I got the impression that she wanted to reciprocate, like she also wanted more time. The Queen has many, many people to see and many, many things to say and that's no mean feat. I think it really is amazing how she does it. I would love to sit down with her over a cup of tea and have a good ol' chinwag!!"*

CHAPTER 23
Mary Percy MBE

WHO: Mary Percy MBE
WHERE: Buckingham Palace
WHEN: 18 February 2004
WHY: Investiture. Receiving MBE

My life has really all been about aviation. I'm eighty-five now and I started working when I was seventeen at the airfield in White Waltham. It was BOAC then (the British Overseas Airways Corporation) and the accounts department for which I worked had been relocated from Bristol, BOAC's original home, because Bristol had been badly bombed during World War II.

This was also the home of the ATA (Air Transport Auxiliary) where many ladies flew the various aircraft in from Canada in World War II. I got to know one or two of them as well as some of the men, but of course they are all now deceased. I bet they would have had some stories to tell!

In 1971, BA (British Airways) was formed when BOAC – who had also previously absorbed BSAA (British South American Airways) – and BEA (British European Airways) merged. This is when I moved to London Heathrow. It was a tiny airport then, nothing like the one we have now.

Mary Percy MBE

I had a great working life and in 1998, at the age of sixty-seven after fifty years of employment, I retired. It was only my actual day job that I retired from, though. I stayed on until I was eighty, continuing my work for a club known in the industry as "The 25-Year Club". For many years I was secretary of The 25-Year Club but in 1976 I became "Lady President, Mary Vincent", the first and only Lady President, not retiring until I reached the age of eighty in 2011.

On 8 January 2004, I received a letter totally out of the blue saying, "Mary Percy, Secretary of The BA 25-Year Club has been awarded an MBE for services to aviation staff in the New Year's Honours list."

I collected my MBE from The Queen at Buckingham Palace on Wednesday, 18 February 2004. I was accompanied by my late husband, Donald, my twin brother Roy and his wife, Valerie. The invitation was signed off with: "I am, Madam, your obedient servant." I loved that!

I also have a lovely poem written by my late husband's son, Ian. Sadly, Ian died very young. He loved calligraphy and so I have the poem, beautifully written by him in my album. I'd like to share it as it means a lot to me.

> *If, like me, you do agree*
> *That Mary's earned her MBE*
> *The only question left to pry*
> *Is what the letters signify*
> *The M for Mary is not so tough*
> *But for B and E there's choice enough*
> *So let's not try to be too clever*
> *We'll keep it simple*
> *Mary Best Ever*

WHAT THE QUEEN SAID TO ME...

"You have worked for a long time for the airline. I do understand."

I said yes, and the conversation bit was over but I think when The Queen had said "I do understand", it was more about The Queen understanding the longevity of my work. It was like she related to me, having herself been in her job for so long.

SUM UP THE QUEEN IN ONE PARAGRAPH:

"The Queen was very approachable. I felt that if I had met her in the street she would have talked to me, or to anyone for that matter. She seemed to be very interested, and she seemed to have an unspoken understanding."

"Just as a little extra to my story... and, I guess a 'perk of the job', I was incredibly lucky and fortunate to have flown on Concorde supersonic from London Heathrow to La Guardia, New York, and then subsonic on to Miami. In the USA, they didn't allow Concorde to fly supersonic due to the sonic boom, so it had to fly a little slower over land. Concorde was fast. It could fly at Mach 2 and I recall it took around three hours and thirty minutes to get from London to New York. On a normal plane it was around seven to eight hours."

CHAPTER 24
Catharina Reynolds OBE

WHO: Catharina Reynolds OBE
WHERE: Buckingham Palace
WHEN: May 2006
WHY: To receive an OBE for services to the London Olympic and Paralympic Games bid

I like to call it "My Accidental Golden Age" because, quite literally, I fell into the job!

I had been working as a civil servant in HMRC in Reading for twenty years. My job was to deal with import and export duties and calculating tax. One day, the powers that be decided to centralise the department and all the jobs in Reading were going somewhere else. I really didn't want to relocate, and the only post on offer in Reading was a VAT officer and I knew that wasn't for me. I was at a crossroads in my life.

Intrigued as to what it would be like to work in Whitehall I started looking at civil servant posts. I saw a job advertised in the Department of Culture, Media & Sport. The position was in the sports department, helping with their tax breaks. It was a no-brainer. I had the tax background, I loved sport, particularly grass roots sport, I had been a civil servant for many years and I had implemented policy in the past. It all seemed to just work, so I applied.

Catharina Reynolds OBE. (Asya at Able Photography)

I was very excited but also incredibly nervous about the interview. After all, I had been in the same job for twenty years and was very out of practice! When I finally arrived on the 6th floor and pulled myself together, all I had to do was go up two little steps that took me into the room where my interviewers were waiting. Just two little steps!!! And then – yes, you guessed it! – I tripped. I fell flat on my face going into the interview and everybody saw. I just thought at that point – well, I've blown it now. I won't get offered the job. I will just go through the motions, get out, go home and cry. I didn't worry anymore. It was the best thing that could have happened to me as I totally relaxed, resigned to having flunked it.

I landed the job which both surprised and thrilled me. I started on 2 June 2002, just after The Queen's Golden Jubilee, and I left just after The Queen's Diamond Jubilee in 2012. It was tough though; I really had to muddle my way through in that first week!

The first thing my boss showed me was a report detailing the cost and benefits of London hosting the Olympic and Paralympic Games in 2012. He informed me, to my surprise, that this was also my area of policy but not to worry as it was going to be too costly and it was unlikely that the other departments would support a bid. He continued, and informed me there was a meeting that coming Friday to discuss the potential bid and could I make sure everyone was ok!

Talk about in at the deep end! I had no idea, really, about what I was doing and, having been told that there would be representatives from every department, I felt rather out of my depth. I went home and cried my eyes out that night, thinking that I just wasn't cut out for the job. Handling a high level meeting in your first week was completely daunting.

On the Friday of the meeting, many representatives turned up. It became apparent that some of the representatives wanted the bid to happen. The Mayor's office (under

Ken Livingstone) and the BOA (British Olympic Association) were very keen.

This was the start of a very big turnaround, and I think it was Tessa Jowell who voiced that it would be good for us as a country. Tessa then went on to speak to Tony Blair, our then Prime Minister, and, I think, together with support from the BOA and the Mayor, they decided that we should put in a bid for the London 2012 Olympic and Paralympic Games.

That was when our Department had to start the hard work. We had all the research to do, report facts and figures, organise a tour of the suggested area. (I have to say, this took a massive amount of imagination. The whole proposed site was polluted. It stank. There were piles of fridges and scaffolding everywhere. It really was a dumping ground, and very hard to imagine it as a prime site for an Olympic Games.)

That was it! I was now part of the team that got everything together to support the bid and after a lot of hard work and late nights that bid became a reality. Thinking back, it was always a struggle. Right up until the last, everyone thought Paris would get it. New York had issues with land which gave us a glimmer of hope in that, at least we may be able to beat them, but Paris? Paris was favourite. 6 July 2005 was the official announcement and – Wow! What a result! – we had won and, as they say, the rest is history.

I was nominated for the OBE because I had been on that government team from the word "Go". I received the OBE (my friend and colleague received an MBE) for all the work I had done from the outset. I think the two of us were some of the only ones that had been there for the entire duration, from a definite "no" to a definite "yes".

That's why I call it "My Accidental Golden Age". I was so fortunate to, quite literally, fall into the job one week before the massive turnaround that occurred, and be part of the team that made the successful bid for the London Olympic and Paralympic Games.

When the letter arrived to say I had been nominated for an OBE I was shocked and overwhelmed. I had to wait until the New Year before I could tell people why! But the time eventually came. The honours ceremony took place in May 2006 and I was allowed to invite three people. I invited my husband, mother-in-law and my younger son. (Luckily for me, my elder son was abroad at the time which made the decision a little easier.)

My mother-in-law had been a massive help to me whilst I had this job as I had worked long hours and she had done a lot for me at home. It felt right to invite her, and she was thrilled to be going to Buckingham Palace and to see The Queen.

On the day, we had problems with traffic and the timing was cut very fine. Luckily, the limousine driver (yes, we had a limousine that was a total surprise to me and a surprise I was incredibly embarrassed about I hasten to add) drove us the back route into London and we arrived just in the nick of time. We were actually the very last car to be let into the palace!

My family were ushered in one direction, and I was told to ascend the grand staircase into a room full of people who were also receiving awards. The equerries were incredibly friendly, and they went through all the rules and the etiquette. I thought it clever how they appear to be asking you, but in fact they were telling you, how to behave. You will not turn your back…

I was all lined up and ready to go. A long queue, then a short queue, then it's stage left, go forward, meet, reverse, curtsey, exit stage right. Funny how you remember these things. So I went forward, shook The Queen's hand very gently and, as she pinned the award on me, she said…

WHAT THE QUEEN SAID TO ME…

"You were there from the start. Well done!"

It was a statement more than a question and I was trying hard to search for an appropriate response. I gathered my thoughts and realised that, yes, I had joined the journey at an early stage. So I said, with a proud smile, "Yes, I was." From that point it was a blur and, for the life of me, I cannot remember exactly what she said. I was so keen to get everything right and remember all the etiquette, that my hearing seemed to suddenly disappear! My moment with The Queen was over in a flash but the clear memory is forever imprinted in my mind.

After the awards I sat next to Lord Sebastian Coe and he also said "Well done!" to me. This was the icing on the cake and it rounded off the day very nicely.

SUM THE QUEEN UP IN ONE PARAGRAPH:

"She is the calmest person. When you think that she has to perform in front of all these people, she doesn't ever appear nervous. She has all these protocols but I never felt like she was judging me in any way. I felt like I really wanted to get it right for her, like she deserved that I get it right. She is unassuming, very friendly, approachable and she does a big smile and looks you right in the eye. A wonderful lady."

CHAPTER 25

Mike Sweeney CBE

WHO: Mike Sweeney CBE

Chairman, Henley Royal Regatta, 1993–2014

WHERE: Buckingham Palace

WHEN: June 2006

WHY: An audience with The Queen

In 1851, Prince Albert, Queen Victoria's Consort, became the Regatta's first Royal Patron. This makes him a key historical figure to the Henley Royal Regatta (HRR).

There are many, many trophies in the Regatta but sometimes there needs to be another. This can be for a number of reasons. Back in 2004, we decided that the Britannia Trophy, a base level coxed four event for both students and club crews, was getting too dominated by the students. Students were able to train whenever they wanted to, but the club crews were losing out as they were mainly working guys who just didn't have the time to train so much. We decided to split the group and instead of having one thirty-two boat event for both groups, we would have two sixteen boat events; one for the students and one for the club crews. The Britannia would remain as the club crews' trophy and a new event would be created for the student fours.

For two years we ran the new event as "The Student Fours" which proved itself as a

Mike Sweeney CBE

success. Now that the event was established, we started to look for a challenge trophy along with a new title for the event. In 2004 Imperial College London (IC) won the inaugural Student Four event. They were very excited when they found out we were looking to give a trophy for this event and they made it clear that they wanted to call it "The Imperial Challenge Trophy".

Unfortunately for them we don't do that. We have a certain protocol and tend to have local Henley names like the Temple Cup etc, names appropriate to the Regatta. We looked at our options and decided to call it the Prince Albert Challenge Cup.

Although Prince Albert wasn't a patron or a benefactor of Imperial College London there was still a connection. If you think about where The Albert Memorial is situated, it is right beside Imperial College London. Prince Albert was associated with and supported the creation of Imperial College London so, as far as the college was concerned, Prince Albert was also a major person in its history. And, as far as the Henley Royal Regatta was concerned, Prince Albert had given us the rights to use the word Royal in the Henley Royal Regatta. That was the connection and, with The Queen being a patron of Imperial College London at the time, it all came together.

The college agreed and they commissioned the renowned silversmith, Hector Miller, to create a beautiful trophy. The Prince Albert Challenge Cup has now been raced for since 2006.

Not surprisingly, in 2006 Imperial College London were really keen for The Queen to come to the Henley Royal Regatta to present the trophy for the first time. The last time she had been to the Regatta was in 1948 when she was Princess Elizabeth. In fact the Princess Elizabeth Challenge Cup is the most sought after school trophy in the world. It is such a fantastic trophy!

Unfortunately for both the Henley Royal Regatta and Imperial College, The Queen is always away in Balmoral early July and never – or very rarely – does any official functions during that time. I can't remember who pushed for it the most, us or Imperial College, but it was arranged and agreed that the four of us – Sir Richard Sykes (Rector of Imperial College London), Hector Miller (silversmith), Richard Goddard (Henley Royal Regatta Secretary) and myself – would have an audience with The Queen at Buckingham Palace. Imperial College London would officially hand over the trophy to the Henley Royal Regatta in The Queen's presence. This was great news and lovely that all the connections had come together.

So, in June 2006 we all arrived. The trophy was promptly taken away from us so it could be positioned in the room for when we entered, where The Queen was waiting. Her role was to preside over proceedings and to be part of the presentation of the trophy. It came to our turn and the four of us entered the room where The Queen was waiting on her own.

It is just an observation really, but it was quite surprising to find her on her own as I thought she may have had someone in there with her. I would say we must have been in there for at least ten minutes, possibly fifteen, chatting about the event in a lovely relaxed way. Her Majesty asked many questions to the four of us including…

WHAT THE QUEEN SAID TO ME…

"How are preparations going for the Regatta?"
"Why the 'Prince Albert' trophy?" "What is the background to it?" "How popular is this event?" "Why the involvement of IC?"

Everything went to perfection until it came to the time of leaving. The four of us had previously been told of the etiquette of backing out of the room, and never turning your back on Her Majesty. We all proceeded to reverse to the door with caution. It was opened by somebody from the outside and we were literally nearly out of the door when Her Majesty said,

"*Oh! What about the trophy?* "

It is quite big and heavy and it was sitting on the pedestal next to her. She had clearly realised we should have been taking it with us. So, in response to her question and for some reason unbeknown to me, I blurted out, "Oh, don't worry, Your Majesty. One of your… er…um… Gremlins will sort it out for us!"

As the door closed in front of me, I wondered where all that had come from! What on earth possessed me to say that? Gremlins! Really? Gremlins! I had looked at The Queen briefly and I know she was smiling, but I was so mortified I didn't know if she actually said anything. And it was going oh so well! A great memory.

SUM THE QUEEN UP IN ONE PARAGRAPH:

"I think she is an absolutely wonderful person and a total professional in what she does. She's good at talking to people and dealing with people. She puts people at their ease and I think she could have a conversation with anybody. She just has a knack of keeping a conversation flowing which I think most of us would find incredibly hard to do when meeting total strangers. "

Mike and Richard with the Prince Albert Cup at HRR in 2015

CHAPTER 26
Judge the Poet

WHO: Judge the Poet
WHERE: The Ritz Hotel, London
WHEN: 6 December 2006
WHY: Performing at The Queen's 80th Birthday

For many years I have been, as far as I am aware, the world's only spontaneous poet. There are some rap artists that do something similar but, as far as poetry is concerned, I am told I am the only one.

In a nutshell I make up poems "on the spot".

For a quarter of a century I have performed all around the world at events and occasions, in theatres, on radio and on television. Audience members give me a mixture of random words and ideas and, there and then, I create and recite a poem using all of those words and ideas. There is no time delay, I do it immediately, and the poems always rhyme and make sense. Also, the poem will always be relevant to the occasion. The audiences I have created poems for range from stag parties to The Queen and everything in between.

Judge the Poet

As a child I used to make up poems and even sometimes speak in rhyme! It took a while until I realised that everyone else didn't do this. I was certainly already doing it in primary school and then, in secondary school, I started to realise I had something unique. It seemed like everybody else knew before me that this was something I had a particular talent for. To me, it was just my life – this was just me, what was the fuss about? It was when I eventually realised for myself that this was something different that I had to start working at it. I suppose it is like when you realise you can run faster than other people or you can play a musical instrument particularly well. That is when you know you have to start practising everyday to make the most of it. Once I'd accepted that I had a fairly unusual ability or talent, I began working incredibly hard to improve and perfect it. I am still doing that today!

In the realms of entertainment and performing I am well known for what I do. This is how I got to do what I do in some venues where The Queen happened to be.

It is not a given that when you are at The Queen's events you will automatically get to meet and talk with The Queen. On the contrary. There are so many people wanting to meet Her Majesty at these places that inevitably there will be some people who leave disappointed. There have been three occasions where I was performing at one of The Queen's events, but only one where I properly met and was able to talk with Her.

The two other events were still amazing occasions and I felt fortunate to be at them. The first one, I was booked by The Queen, along with a number of other performers, to be at a garden party at Buckingham Palace in 2006. This was part of The Queen's 80th Birthday events. The second, I was invited to entertain at an event for a number of VIPs at Kensington Palace in 2011. While I crossed paths with The Queen on this occasion it was not when I had my main conversation.

The meeting when this did happen was The Queen's private 80th Birthday Party. This took place at the Ritz Hotel in London in December 2006. The Queen had already had a year's worth of celebrating her birthday with lots of public engagements. This event was a much more private affair. I would guess that there were about 300 guests. Heads of State, Dukes, Lords and Ladies. I tried to imagine what The Queen's private phone book looked like and I am sure everyone in it was there. I was there, of course, as part of the entertainment.

Doing what I do, I introduced myself to various groups of people and created poems for them. That is what I was there for, to work, to entertain the guests. That was my role. I was not particularly expecting to meet and talk with The Queen herself that day. In fact it was rather out of the blue that the Queen's cousin, a lady very familiar with my work, approached me and asked me to accompany her across the room. I suddenly realised she was taking me to meet The Queen. So it was at the Ritz, at The Queen's 80th Birthday party, when I had my conversation with The Queen.

Her cousin reminded The Queen what I do and suggested I create a poem for The Queen. I asked The Queen if she would approve and she warmly agreed. The family members and friends that happened to be nearby joined in. I asked three or four of the guests, The Queen being the first, what word or phrase they would like to choose. I trust I'm not breaking the Official Secrets Act or any similar agreement by divulging that, when asked, The Queen's nomination was...

WHAT THE QUEEN SAID TO ME...

"The Ritz"

I thanked Her Majesty and asked some of the other members of the group for their words or ideas.

Based on the words and ideas the whole group gave me I recited an on-the-spot poem. I tried to make it appropriate to Her Majesty in the presence of her friends and family. I included ideas about her long service, her friends and being there at The Ritz. While using all the various words I had been given, I tried to put in as much content as I could.

In a setting such as this, it seemed nice and fitting to make a poem in tribute to the guest of honour. It was her birthday and her party after all! I tried to include some ideas I had picked up from the guests that day. There was certainly, in the room, a sense of thanks, loyalty and appreciation to a well-respected lady. The Queen and her friends seemed to be very pleased and I did receive smiles and applause from the whole party.

Many people have asked me if I was particularly nervous at this event because of who my host and audience member was. Particularly when I was asked to talk and perform directly for her. I hope I don't sound too big-headed or blasé when I say that I wasn't. You see, unlike many entertainers, I do not have a script. I always have to think on my feet and be, as sports people always say, in the zone. So for me every audience is equally nerve wracking! I am used to it and actually quite like it. I obviously could not have this career otherwise.

I have to say another reason I was not nervous was The Queen herself. Her own self, her own personality. She genuinely has a very warm and charismatic presence that puts you at ease. I would say this of only a handful of people I have met in my life, even those in high positions, but The Queen really can light up a room as surely as a light bulb. Nelson Mandela was a very strong example of someone with this quality. The Queen is one of those rare people who can meet with a crowd and make all the individuals feel they have been noticed. In a different world, she would have made an excellent performer! I felt more at ease with The Queen than I have with many other people I have met and performed for.

SUM UP THE QUEEN IN ONE PARAGRAPH:

"The Queen has obviously been given her job by circumstance of birth and, whatever your feelings about the job itself, she is ideal for it. I cannot imagine another person fitting that role more successfully. She has a lot of people to meet and somehow, I believe, everybody feels like they have made a connection. So she does her difficult job exceptionally well. The Queen is very clearly as sharp as a razor and still has amazing stamina. Her intelligence is striking and obvious to anyone who meets her."

I have created a poem for this book about The Queen.

Exceptional lady, historic tradition;
A unifying heart devoted to her mission.
A loving nation looks on with stories to tell
Of a sincere life of service, lived long and well.

CHAPTER 27
Moira Logie

WHO: Moira Logie
WHERE: Oxford
WHEN: 2007
WHY: Royal Opening of the Children's Hospital and West Wing at the John Radcliffe

I guess I was in the right place at the right time.

I had gone to work at the Oxford Radcliffe Hospital's NHS Trust in 2006 as Director of Operations running cardiac, the cancer centre and other emergency services. I was also the project director of Oxford's new Heart Centre, a massive project which, after two years, was halfway to being completely built when The Queen came to open the Children's Hospital and West Wing.

The Oxford Radcliffe Hospital's West Wing was the new home for all the neurological services that had previously been located in the old Radcliffe Infirmary. The brand new Children's Hospital was desperately needed and these two departments were the reason for this Royal visit.

On a personal level, I had not actually been involved in these two facilities but, as a

Marie Logie (photo courtesy Mary Smith)

result of my involvement with the other aspects of the hospital, our team were invited to the opening. On top of that, which in itself was great news, we were told we would also get the chance to meet and speak with The Queen.

The whole event was a huge affair based in the atrium of the Children's Hospital and West Wing. There were hundreds of people both inside and outside, lining the roads, banks, footpaths. It was an amazing sight.

The day started with some formalities with Her Majesty meeting key people such as the Chief Executive and the Head of the Medical School at the University. We, in the meantime, were all in our little pod-like groups in the atrium chatting amongst ourselves. The day continued with the Royal Party being shown around some of the key facilities in both buildings, after which they would enter the atrium where we were waiting. There was definitely an energy in the room which you could feel throughout the time The Queen and the Royal party were there. The Queen unveiled a small plaque, and she gave a short talk. Then it was time for her and Prince Philip to work their way through the various pods of people.

There was somebody introducing her to the various people in the groups, and I knew The Queen was getting closer. Then, after a short time she was with us. It did seem incredibly sudden and I quickly realised someone was pointing at me and saying, "This is Moira Logie. Moira is involved in building the Heart Centre, our new services for cardiac patients."

I was suddenly overwhelmed with the protocol, and I did my best attempt at a curtsey. I hope I did okay! I shook The Queen's white gloved hand very gently, as that is how you are told to do it. The Queen then proceeded to say to me (which I thought was really quite funny)…

WHAT THE QUEEN SAID TO ME...

"The Heart Centre? Hmm... Tell me, are we going to have buildings for every part of the body here in Oxford?"

She was smiling when she said it. Clearly, she thinks on her feet with what I would say was a great but very subtle sense of humour. I replied, chuckling slightly, with, "That's a very amusing point, Ma'am, though I don't think so, as often people present with many problems together so it probably wouldn't work very well. Mind you, for specialist services like the new West Wing, it actually makes a lot of sense."

She replied, smiling:

"Thank you. And you are – all of you – doing a good job."

SUM THE QUEEN UP IN ONE PARAGRAPH:

"She is, and she brings to events, a remarkable symbol of Britishness. I was struck by how petite she was and she had really quite tiny hands. But also she looked me in the eye and she definitely had a twinkle about her. I thought, after probably having just met forty or fifty people that day, it was rather nice to see her personalising each exchange. I was surprised by her powers of endurance."

CHAPTER 28
Ruth Best

WHO: Ruth Best, Office Manager, Committee Office, House of Lords

WHERE: Royal Gallery, House of Lords, London

WHEN: Tuesday, 20 October 2009

WHY: Unveiling of Queen Elizabeth II Portrait Bust

I work in the Committee Office at the House of Lords. We run select committees which undertake investigative inquiries in various subject areas and we produce reports which contain the committee's findings and recommendations to the government. My role is to manage the technical unit and to train and look after the committee assistants who work for the committee clerks.

About nine or ten years ago, the Clerk of the Parliaments – the most senior official in the House of Lords, equivalent to a CEO in a commercial business – decided that the clerks were all rather busy and that there would be other employees who would be perfectly suited and equally able to run a committee.

It was to be a first, but the Clerk of the Parliaments decided to run an internal recruitment process for the post of Clerk of the Works of Art Committee (one of the domestic as opposed to investigative committees). This was an amazing opportunity

Marie Logie (photo courtesy Mary Smith)

and I really wanted to land this role. It was right up my street and so I applied.

Competition was fierce. The role was much sought after and a rather large number of people applied. After a gruelling application process, I was informed that I had been successful and the job was mine. It was fantastic news, absolutely great and I was over the moon.

Fear subsided and excitement rose as I knew I would be working closely with some amazing people including the Curator of the Parliamentary Works of Art Collection and I would be joining in with about half a dozen big meetings throughout the year. Yes, it really was a very exciting time.

The timing was perfect. No sooner had I started, the Works of Art Committee, which is made up of various members of the House of Lords, decided to undertake the biggest project the Committee had ever undertaken. The project was to recreate six huge portraits of the Spanish Armada tapestries. This was a project that was started by Prince Albert in the 19th century. It was now my job to help to make this happen.

A brief look at history: shortly after the 1588 Spanish Armada, Lord Howard of Effingham, serving Admiral of the Armada, commissioned ten tapestries to commemorate the British victory. Sadly, after being housed in many palaces and royal residences, the tapestries perished in a huge fire at the Palace of Westminster in 1834. As luck would have it, a series of engravings were created by the artist John Pine in the 1730s as a sort of business continuum I guess, and it was these engravings that were used to recreate the paintings of the tapestries. I believe these engravings are the only living records of the tapestries left today.

Directly behind the main Lord's Chamber in The House of Lords there is a room called the Prince's Chamber. This room houses many works of art. Inside the Prince's Chamber, there are six huge panels which were created as part of Prince Albert's vision with the sole intention of putting the commissioned Works of Art of the Spanish Armada in them. Unfortunately, by about 1861, only one of the paintings was finished and so only one panel was filled. I believe the Fine Arts Commission ran out of money and that was the end of that. Well, not totally the end, because this is where we came in and the Works of Art Committee, over a hundred years later, was tasked with effectively finishing off Prince Albert's Spanish Armada project.

Funnily enough the "Armada" story does not directly link to my meeting with The Queen. However, without it, my meeting would not have taken place. You see, alongside the Armada project, another project was taking place. That project was the completion of a "Portrait Bust" of The Queen created by a sculptor named Oscar Nemon who died in 1985. Oscar had already created the head and shoulders part of the bust but the Works of Art Committee wanted it to be completed with a plinth. I believe they used the original mould and the project was duly completed over twenty years after Nemon's death.

The Committee thought The Queen might be interested in the Armada story, so I wrote to the palace to ask if The Queen would be interested in officially unveiling the Armada paintings. The Committee also asked if I could include an invitation for The Queen to unveil the bust, so the letter was very much about both.

We didn't have any clue as to whether The Queen would come for one or both or neither so we sat with crossed fingers and we waited. The palace replied and said that Her Majesty and the Duke of Edinburgh would like to come and unveil the portrait bust but The Queen would not be able to unveil the Armada paintings. So, with the invitation accepted, I got to work organising the royal event which we were informed

The Armada paintings at high level in the Prince's Chamber, House of Lords
(©UKParliament)

had to be informal and that a large portion of the guests were to be made up of staff from the House of Lords.

My first thought when The Queen got to me was how really very tiny she was. I think probably just under five foot, but she had the most beautiful, beautiful skin.

WHAT THE QUEEN SAID TO ME...

"So, what do you do?"

I told her, in a very shortened form, about my role in The House of Lords, about the Committee and that I had organised this event.

She listened intently, smiled at me and said, *"Very good."*

SUM UP THE QUEEN IN A PARAGRAPH:

"It was lovely to see her laugh, albeit from afar and she is a wonderful lady. Friendly but serious, and considerate too. It was lovely she had stipulated that regular staff should be at this event, people she would not ordinarily have met. I found that endearing. She showed a lot of thought and I felt she really wanted to ease people's nerves. The Queen was also immaculately turned out, not a crease or wrinkle on her jacket, everything was smooth and I remember thinking: When I get out of the car, I always seem to look rather dishevelled. How does she do it?"

CHAPTER 29

Asghar Majeed

WHO:	Asghar Majeed, Mayor of the Royal Borough of Windsor & Maidenhead 2011–2012
WHERE:	Buckingham Palace and Windsor
WHEN:	2012
WHY:	Loyal Address and Walkabout

As Mayor of the Royal Borough of Windsor & Maidenhead, I was privileged to meet The Queen on a number of occasions.

I remember the very first time I met Her Majesty. She asked me where I was from. I said I was from Yorkshire. She looked at me and said, "No, no. I mean, originally." To which I smiled and said, "Kashmir". This is what ordinary people say and I thought it was nice. She went on to show a genuine interest in my family.

The second time I met Her Majesty was at the Loyal Address at Buckingham Palace. As the Mayor, I was allowed to take five or six guests. I decided to take some of the longest serving councillors we had, and one of them was my fellow ward councillor, Derek Wilson. He was extremely pleased and he went out especially to get a brand new suit, shirt and shoes. Everything. It was a really special day for him. I think he was probably the most excited of us all.

Asghar Majeed

He said to me, "On the day, when you speak to The Queen, can you introduce me to her?" I said, "Yeah, of course I can do that for you."

So the day came and, as is normal procedure on these occasions, Her Majesty enters in through one door at one end of the room and she works her way through the line up and then leaves through the door at the other end of the room. Derek was standing just before me in the line up. The Queen shook hands and chatted with a few of the people in the line up, and then she walked straight past Derek and started talking to me. Poor Derek! I could feel how disappointed he was. It's probably not the best protocol, but I said to The Queen, "I'd really like to introduce you to my fellow councillor, Derek Wilson. He bought a brand new suit and shirt especially, because he really wanted to meet you, Ma'am."

Hats off to her as she did actually turn back, which doesn't normally happen I hasten to add. She looked Derek up and down, gave a wry smile and may have shaken his hand before walking on. Derek was shocked but seriously happy, and later in the day he said to me, "I can't believe you actually said that to The Queen, though she did appear quite amused by the whole thing, didn't she?"

The third time was very brief. It was at an annual parade at Windsor Castle just before the walkabout that was due to take place a couple of days later, to which this fourth story pertains. I just happened to be standing nearby in my full Mayoral Regalia when The Queen came over to me. I think she was with the Scoutmaster. We chatted briefly about the upcoming walkabout that was taking place two or three days later and, as we looked up at the grey sky above, I said, "Ma'am, you're going to have to pray in your Church and I'll have to pray in my mosque for the weather to improve."

She smiled and agreed.

Being Mayor of the Royal Borough in the jubilee year was amazing. The fourth occasion was a special walkabout for The Queen to thank the residents of Windsor for all the support they had given to her and the Royal Family over the years. It was only done this particular year because it was The Queen's Diamond Jubilee.

We arranged to meet The Queen and her entourage outside the gates of Windsor Castle. Her Majesty would arrive by car. She would get out of the car then I would introduce her to a few people. She would then walk down the hill towards Queen Victoria's Statue and then up the steps to the Guildhall where I would introduce her to more people. These were selected people who had a sixty-year anniversary of some form or another, whether it was a sixtieth birthday or a diamond wedding anniversary. They were people who had that sixty-year jubilee connection.

I would give my short, prepared speech and present The Queen with a gift of a pen and then ask her if she'd like a cup of tea. I was advised she would say no to the cup of tea, which is normal practice. She would sign the visitors' book and then she would leave. The chap sitting next to me in the rehearsal said in all the time he had been doing this, and it had been twelve years or so, she always declined the cup of tea.

The rehearsal concluded, we had everything in place and we were good to go.

The day of the walkabout came. I was in my red gown with my Mayoral "pirate's" hat, and I met up with Her Majesty and Prince Philip as planned at the gates of Windsor Castle. I was introducing her to a few people who were standing outside and Prince Philip said to me, "You have a good memory, there. Lots of names to remember."

I smiled and quietly confided in him that I had a little list of names in my pirate's hat because there was no way I could remember that many names. He chuckled and very quickly said, "Oh! You're picking names out of the hat then!" I thought that was quick-witted and very funny.

Anyway, we did the tour as planned and The Queen was really obliging when I mentioned my parents and pointed out where they were. She went over and spoke to them, saying they must be really proud of my sister and me. (My sister was the Mayoress.) My family beamed with pride that day, and it was a very touching moment for me.

We continued on the rather long walk but eventually we got up the hill to the Guildhall, and I made the introductions to all the people sharing their anniversaries that year. I made my little speech and managed to mention Yorkshire five or six times. I am a Yorkshire lad, you see, and I just had to get that in. It was quite a spirited speech, not solemn at all but quick and lively.

I gave The Queen the pen and then came the last question before she left. I asked her if she'd like a cup a Yorkshire Tea. Having been briefed that The Queen's answer would be no, Her Majesty replied with...

WHAT THE QUEEN SAID TO ME...

"Oh! Yes, of course. That would be nice."

I was stunned, thinking, "Err... Whoops!" I was shocked. The Queen had never ever said yes to this offer before. What was I to do?

Passing the buck straightaway, I turned to my colleague Andrew and said. "We need to get four cups of tea, please."

He, too, was stunned, just like a deer in the headlamps. He was startled for a split second, probably wondering how on earth he was going to get four cups of tea to The Queen of England, us having not made a contingency plan for this eventuality. Andrew suddenly turned and – whoosh! – he was off in a flash. It was like "now you see him, now you don't!" The Queen smiled.

There was a bit of chitchat and Prince Philip piped up and said, "Yorkshire Tea? There's no such thing. Tea comes from Ceylon."

So I said to him, "Yeah, Yeah. Um, we've got an area in Ceylon called Yorkshire, and that's where we get our tea from!" He laughed at that.

Luckily a lady named Fiona who does catering for the Mayor, happened to have brought her own Nan's tea set in. Andrew appeared a few minutes later with the tea in Fiona's tea set. We were saved by Fiona and the caterers, because I don't know what we would have done if we had had to give The Queen of England Yorkshire Tea in polystyrene cups! Fiona subsequently called her relatives in Australia or somewhere and shouted. 'The Queen's drinking out of our family china!"

SUM THE QUEEN UP IN ONE PARAGRAPH:

"She is a very lovely lady, very down-to-earth, charming and a very hard worker. I could not have done that job for the last sixty years or so. I think it's a very mentally draining job, but she does it so well."

CHAPTER 30
Fred Simmonds

WHO:	Fred Simmonds, Royal Borough's Mayor's Office, Mace Bearer 1993–2013
WHERE:	Windsor Guildhall
WHEN:	2012 Diamond Jubilee
WHY:	Windsor Walkabout

On The Queen's 80th birthday, I walked with her through Windsor. This was such a great occasion and, for me, a huge privilege. I carried the mace as usual, which is protocol, and we wandered the streets of this beautiful town where The Queen stopped and spoke to many of the residents and visitors that had turned out that day. There were thousands of people around but actually the event wasn't officially scheduled. The Queen has such a following.

Ordinarily, one carries the mace in the normal manner, the right way up. The mace represents The Queen when she is not present. I don't know if you know, but when Her Majesty is present the Mace then becomes redundant. In that situation one carries it upside down. There was a lot of media interest that day and I think some of the television crews thought I had made some kind of unthinkable mistake! Look, he's got it upside down!! I thought the German television crews were not particularly well informed so, in my broken German, I told them that the Mace is a sort of substitute

Fred Simmonds

Fred with the Mace upside down

and it is upright when The Queen is not present but as soon as she is there in person, the Mace gets turned upside down. I think I repeated that sentence to many journalists that day.

The thing is with me, as I am there in a professional manner, I get to be in Her Majesty's presence and company but tend not to be there in a conversational manner; it's not something you do to approach The Queen. She has nodded and she certainly recognises me, but we have never chatted so to speak.

However, there was one incident that day where she did speak to me but it was a bit of a disaster on my part. The Queen was signing the visitors book in the Guildhall after the walkabout, and I was with her making sure that things went smoothly when she turned to me totally out of the blue, and asked...

WHAT THE QUEEN SAID TO ME...

"What is the date today?"

Do you know, I just couldn't think! My mind had gone completely blank and, to make the matter a whole lot worse, I suddenly saw Prince Philip come rushing across. He must have noticed my hesitation and he made an incredibly quick decision to step in and save the day. He then told both of us what the date was! I was so embarrassed but I vaguely recall a slight smile on both their faces.

"A nice tradition that used to happen is that on State Visits to Windsor we would have to present the Visiting Head of State with a 'Scroll of Welcome'. The councillors used to gather and I used to carry the Mace into Windsor Castle. I had special permission from The Queen to do this. I would present the Scroll to the Visiting Head and the Mayor, standing behind me, would make his welcome.

It was a very lovely thing to do but, unfortunately and, along with many other traditions, we have lost it. I find this loss really quite sad."

Fred with The Queen and Prince Philip at Buckingham Palace in Legoland in 2003

LEGOLAND

There was actually a funny situation once with Her Majesty. The Assistant Mayor's Officer and myself went to Legoland, 11 June 2003 it was, where the Royal Family had gone on an official visit to see the miniature Buckingham Palace that had been built there.

The day had gone well without a glitch and, just prior to the Royal party leaving, the Mayor at the time, who was disabled, announced that he needed something. I can't remember exactly what it was but I think it may have been a raincoat or an umbrella. My colleague and I went to get it and were about to return to the Mayor. We came out of the building into the actual courtyard where the Royal car was waiting to take the Royal party home. The timing was impeccable! We appeared unexpectedly, just as The Queen was approaching the car. The police on duty saw us and told us to wait where we were. There was no time to get us out and no place to hide.

My colleague said in a panic, "What do we do, Fred?" and I, trying to think on my feet, said, "Just stand here and if she notices us, we just give a nod and bow."

The amusing thing was that she spotted us straightaway and I know for sure she clocked what had happened. We were alone, stuck on this path, nowhere to go and she saw the funny side. She made very brief eye contact and I saw her laugh. It was like she thought: "Ha! I caught you out." My picture is in the *Daily Express* for that one.

SUM THE QUEEN UP IN ONE PARAGRAPH:

"I think she is a jovial, gentle and very nice person. I have noticed through my time serving her that she doesn't forget a lot – The Queen and also Prince Phillip. He has got such a great memory. They really don't forget much at all."

CHAPTER 31

Elizabeth Hodgkin

WHO:	Elizabeth Hodgkin, Mayor of Henley-on-Thames 2009–2010 & 2012–2013
WHERE:	Henley Business School at the University of Reading
WHEN:	2012 the year of The Queen's Diamond Jubilee
WHY:	Three-County Diamond Jubilee Party

As part of The Queen's Diamond Jubilee Celebrations The Queen wanted to visit every county in the country. However, that was proving to be a bit of a hard task so the powers that be decided three counties should work together on one event. The Lord-Lieutenants of Oxfordshire, Buckinghamshire and Berkshire organised a River Pageant for Her Majesty and The Duke of Edinburgh to enjoy with approximately 4,000 guests. The pageant was to take place at the Henley Business School in Henley on Thames on Monday 25 June 2015 and I, in my role as Mayor of Henley at the time, was invited to formally meet The Queen.

It's funny how things happen. I thought I would just be a guest and that I may get a glimpse of Her Majesty at a distance if I was really lucky. However, the day before the pageant I was told I had been selected to formally meet The Queen! I was really quite nervous and suddenly I was also very worried about my outfit as I was not going to be dressed in my Mayoral Regalia.

Elizabeth Hodgkin

I am so glad I decided to wear something I had bought for my son's wedding a few years before. I did consider going out and buying a frock I had seen in the window of a shop in Henley but I just didn't have enough time. The circumstances paid off. I saw three people wearing the same lovely pink dress I had seen in the shop in town! I believe one lady actually went home to change. I really felt for her as she had probably spent ages deliberating and debating and finally deciding on what to wear just as I

Elizabeth Hodgkin just after speaking with The Queen at Henley Business School.
(Thanks to Charlotte Snowden for the Henley Standard)

had. So there I was with one day to go, about to meet The Queen of England; worried, nervous and hugely excited. I couldn't wait until the following day.

WHAT THE QUEEN SAID TO ME...

"I'm so sorry about the traffic problems that I have caused in Henley."

I replied with. "Not at all." Afterwards, when I thought about what she had said, I remembered that in fact she had arrived by boat so had not directly caused any traffic problems in Henley whatsoever!

It was over in a blink. It was a huge lead up to such a tiny conversation but I will always remember it as the highlight of my term as Mayor of Henley-on-Thames, and one of those very special moments that are quite rare but we sometimes get in life if we are really lucky.

Directly after The Queen had spoken to me, suddenly The Duke of Edinburgh was there. He shook my hand, lifted up my Mayoral chain and said, nodding: "Hmmm... Nice badge!" I managed to hold in the laugh I so desperately wanted to let out and did a polite grin.

SUM THE QUEEN UP IN ONE PARAGRAPH:

"She is quite small and getting more and more like Her Majesty Queen Elizabeth the Queen Mother in the way she looks and behaves. Her skin is incredibly beautiful and she has very, very sparkly eyes. I also love her hats. They are truly amazing."

CHAPTER 32

Shamsul Shelim

WHO:	Shamsul Shelim
WHERE:	Windsor
WHEN:	October 2012
WHY:	Unveiling of the Diamond Jubilee Statue

The reason for my part in this whole event was because I, as a local businessman and as the owner of The Viceroy of Windsor Restaurant, was invited by the former Mayor Asghar Majeed to be one of the sponsors of the Diamond Jubilee Tribute Sculpture. This beautiful sculpture was made for the town centre to represent The Queen's sixty years on the throne and I was invited to the unveiling of the sculpture.

There was a competition held by the Windsor & Eton Society that asked local schools to come up with a design. There were many designs including stained glass windows and a bronze horse that I can remember, but it was a fourteen-year-old, Year 11 pupil from Windsor Girls' School, Caroline Basra, who created the winning design. A piece of art with 59 stainless steel spheres and one glass sphere on the top.

WHAT THE QUEEN SAID TO ME...

"Whereabouts in Windsor is your restaurant?"

Shamsul Shelim

I had to be honest and so told her: "Your Majesty, you did go to my restaurant once. Well, up to the front door of it anyway, but you didn't go in!"

"*W*ell, how come I didn't go in?"

So I told her the reason. "You were there in 2006 when you officially opened the East Berkshire College in St. Leonards Road. Well, my restaurant is opposite the College. When your car stopped for you to get out and start the tour, it stopped right outside my restaurant's front doors! Unfortunately for me, you got out and walked

Above: 60 spheres for 60 years – the sculpture in the centre of Windsor

Left: Shelim shaking hands with The Queen in 2012

the opposite way, over towards the college. The police had actually asked me to lock the doors to my restaurant for security."

"*Oh. Well how long have you been there?*"

I told her I had just recently had my Silver Jubilee only a couple of months before.

"*25 years,*" she said. "*I hope to see you stay there longer.*"

My last words to her were: "I am hoping to be there as long as I can, but it is a long way to the Diamond Jubilee for me," and we both laughed.

SUM THE QUEEN UP IN ONE PARAGRAPH:

"*The Queen was incredibly polite and the feeling I got from her was that she really wanted to explore and meet more people from all societies and all walks of life. She was so very nice to talk to and she listens intently to every word you say.*"

CHAPTER 33
Bernie Aitken

WHO: Bernie Aitken

WHERE: Coworth Park Hotel, Ascot

WHEN: End of 2012

WHY: A friend of The Queen's 90th birthday party

My name is Bernie, and I am a piper. In fact, I teach the bagpipes at a lovely school in Newbury which is where this story originates.

The grandmother of one of my students is a very dear friend of Queen Elizabeth II and she was hosting a 90th birthday party at the Coworth Park Hotel in Ascot. It was towards the end of 2012 and The Queen was a guest at the party. My friend's grandson and I were invited to play the bagpipes as part of the entertainment.

We were playing as The Queen entered the hotel. It was a great pleasure and I know my student enjoyed it as much as I did. I had no idea that later that day The Queen would send for me to "have a chat"!

It's a rather unusual feeling when The Queen makes eye contact with you. Because I was playing my bagpipes and trying desperately hard not to mess up my music, I could not acknowledge her in return! I did manage to keep playing and The Queen listened to us for a while. I know she was smiling throughout at both myself and my student, the birthday girl's grandson.

Bernie Aitken

Bernie Aitken in full regalia

After a little while, The Queen disappeared into the party and I went to a private room, thinking it was all over. However, a little while later, a member of staff appeared and told me very matter-of-factly that The Queen had asked specifically to see me. When I was introduced I shook her hand and, very naturally, we started talking about the bagpipes...

WHAT THE QUEEN SAID TO ME...

"How long have you been piping?"

"You must have a lot of puff to blow them!"

"It is so lovely to see a female piper."

I answered all of her questions and we had a very nice chat. It was a very special moment. I did want to ask her if she'd like to have a go on the pipes but I couldn't bring myself to say it. If I had asked though, I feel she probably would have laughed and dismissed the offer with a great deal of tact! The Queen was very easy to talk to and it really was lovely to just chat with her.

SUM THE QUEEN UP IN ONE PARAGRAPH:

"What mesmerised me was how beautiful and radiant she looked, and how relaxed she was. I could have gone on talking to her for hours. I feel privileged to have had the opportunity to meet her. The fact that it was The Queen herself who had asked to see me specifically was absolutely amazing, and it will stay with me forever. She is just lovely."

CHAPTER 34

Robin Williams MBE

WHO:	Robin Williams MBE
WHERE:	Windsor Castle
WHEN:	April 2013
WHY:	Investitute, receiving my MBE

My name is Robin Williams. All of my life I have been involved in rowing in one way or another. As a child I rowed at Monmouth School and as a teenager, living in Chepstow, I rowed for Wales. I rowed for London University and eventually rowed for GB until the early 1990s.

After that I went on to coach. I cannot believe it is twenty-five years or so now of coaching. For eleven years of that twenty-five, I coached the Cambridge Boat Race crew which was a wonderful experience and, since then, I have been a coach on the GB team.

In 2010 I started coaching a female GB coxless pair, Helen Glover and Heather Stanning. These two amazingly talented girls won the very first gold medal for Great Britain at the 2012 London Olympic and Paralympic Games and repeated their success in 2016 in Rio.

I guess I have been quite lucky in that with my career I have met a number of royals, a number of times. One of the first times was when I rowed for Wales at

Robin Williams (Intersport Images Rowing)

Robin Williams in the nylon GB commonwealth games kit in 1986

the 1986 Commonwealth Games which were in Scotland that year. This was, of course, when rowing was part of the Commonwealth Games. I came fouth in Scotland which is just about the worst place to be for an athlete. A medal was not meant for me that year and I felt rubbish. However, socially, it was actually a very good time.

Pretty much the whole Royal Family were there in Scotland to watch the Commonwealth Games including The Queen and Princess Diana, and there was a real buzz about the place. There were a number of social events throughout. Even Prince Andrew came to an athlete disco one night. He was dating Koo Stark in those days and we all danced together. It was a great time. There was also a garden party at Holyrood House, hosted by The Royal Family, and athletes from the Welsh Team were invited too. I duly attended.

Fortunately, I did seem to have some kind of contact with nearly all of the royals at some point throughout the day so, for me, it was a really nice memorable event. My introductions did include a few moments with Princess Diana which I know is not what this book or this interview is about but, weirdly, it does have a relevance when I met The Queen years later.

I deliberately positioned myself into a place where I thought a meeting might happen. The Welsh team were all in these bright red nylon blazers that gave you an electric shock when you touched them, and we wore equally not very nice cream nylon trousers. But kit didn't matter. I was going to meet Princess Diana. So long as I didn't give her an electric shock, all would be great. I waited patiently thinking of all the wonderful things I could say.

Princess Diana was finally there in front of me. She shook my hand and, looking at my kit, she said something like, "Oh hello, and what do you do?"

And then came my wonderful, amazing reply. All those chatty things I could have said and what came out of my mouth was, "Err, uh, oh. Ummm... I'm a rower... err." Seriously!!

Within a moment she had said, "Oh! That's nice," and she walked on.

You have that critical moment where you could say something really smart or funny or interesting. That moment – my moment – had well and truly gone. I had really fluffed it. I'd blown it! My first and last time when I could have spoken to Princess Diana and I have to say... I was gutted. Oh well, lesson learned!

I did meet The Queen at the Commonwealth Games, but it was a very informal chitchat in a rather big group so I didn't get her personal attention. The biggie, the official meeting with The Queen, was when I received my MBE.

On the day of the investiture, my mind skipped back many times to my disastrous meeting with Princess Diana. I regarded this as my lesson, and I was not going to duplicate the mistake I had made over twenty-five years previously.

Robin Williams MBE with Wife Judy outside Buckingham Palace on the day of the investiture

WHAT THE QUEEN SAID TO ME...

"Oh, very well done with the Olympics. I've had both your girls up here just a short while ago."

I had missed the girls' moment as I was in another room waiting my turn. Being Jubilee year also in 2012, I said, "Oh! May I just say, Ma'am, congratulations on your jubilee."

There was wonderful expression in The Queen's eyes, suggesting she was rather surprised and also delighted that I had brought up something relevant.

"Oh, thank you very much."

"Well, I felt really rather sorry for you on the Royal Barge that day, with the weather as it was. It must have been horrible."

The Queen then said, as her face lit up:

"Oh, yes. It was rather cold on the river."

SUM UP THE QUEEN IN ONE PARAGRAPH:

"There is most certainly a warmth to The Queen and I felt I could talk to her. She is very dignified and warm and able to say the right thing, I never felt she was just filling in time and she certainly appears to put people at ease. You cannot ignore who she is but it would be so good to have a cup of tea and a proper chat. I am sure many people feel this way. The Queen's speech is so very different to how she is in real life and I do not think it depicts her wonderfully warm personality. The Queen is a very sweet and special lady. I think the whole Royal Family add something to the British people, particularly with the sense of history that Royalty brings."

CHAPTER 35
Helen Glover MBE &
Heather Stanning MBE

WHO: Helen Glover MBE & Heather Stanning MBE
WHERE: Windsor Castle
WHEN: April 2013
WHY: Investiture, receiving their MBEs

HELEN:

Ever since I was little and all through growing up I was sporty, very sporty. I had been successful throughout my school days and had got to international standard at cross country. Hockey was also a sport I happened to be very good at.

When I went to university in Cardiff I played sport really just for fun and recreation. None of my family had ever rowed and when I finished university at twenty-one I still hadn't started rowing.

It was my Mum actually, who unbeknown to me at the time, kick started the whole rowing thing for me by telling me about a TV sport talent show called "Sporting Giants". I applied and to my surprise and a bit of luck I scraped in.

I was just coming to the end of my PGCE – Postgraduate Certificate in Education. My sensible side argued with my competitive side but I didn't want to let this opportunity pass me by. I wanted to get to the Olympics and that was my sole aim!

Helen Glover and Heather Stanning (Intersport Images Rowing)

So I moved to Bath and started rowing as part of the GB Rowing Team Start Programme. Training was part-time alongside my then full time teaching job and that is where Heather comes into the story.

Paul Stannard, our coach in Bath, decided to put the two of us together, another of my ambitions was to trial for the team in a boat with Heather.

The wonderful Robin Williams became our coach and he took us on our incredible journey.

The London 2012 Olympic and Paralympic Games were the first Olympics we raced in but I remember watching the 2008 Beijing Olympics literally just as I had started rowing, we are talking weeks. I watched and thought – I want to do that. That was my sole drive. And I did. I have been told I am the only person that has made it to Olympic gold just four years after getting in a boat for the first time. I also hold the record for the shortest time, two years, from getting onto the GB team and winning a medal at the World Championships. That was in 2010.

Winning the Olympic Gold at Dorney Lake felt incredible. We loved and savoured every moment. We could not have done it without Robin. He was, and still is, amazing. It was also the very first GB Olympic Gold which made it that bit sweeter.

Heather, Robin and myself were all told we would be receiving an MBE. I guess the beauty of the MBE is that it is not your doing – somebody else has bestowed it on you, someone else has thought that you should receive this for the effort and work you have done – it was a lovely bonus, for all three of us.

HEATHER:
I have always been sporty but didn't start rowing until I was nineteen years old. Quite late in some people's eyes. I wasn't really that serious about rowing. I just wanted to do something a little different and have a sporty social life! I had not really had the opportunity before to try rowing and that is ultimately why I picked that sport. People had said in the past I should try because I am tall at 5ft 11in and so I joined the boat club at the university I attended and started. Much to my surprise a rowing coach named Paul Stannard spotted me and I came into the GB Rowing Team Start Programme where I teamed up with Helen. We were a perfect fit, partly because we were similar in height, but also because we were tied to our careers. We could meet up and train evenings and weekends only.

In 2007, I had become the under twenty-three world champion in the Coxless Pairs with a talented rower named Olivia Whitlam. I had never actually considered rowing as a career, I had only ever considered a career in the military.

The military was my dream, my passion. I had always wanted to join and that was my ambition. I duly went off to Sandhurst Military Academy for my Officer training. A year was spent there and I put rowing on the back burner. I rowed at Army level and kind of left it at that.

The day I was Commissioned just happened to be the day of the opening ceremony at the 2008 Beijing Olympics. I watched. Olivia, who I had won the World U23 Championships with was there in Beijing and I wasn't! Actually that was a moment for me. It made me stop in my tracks. I absolutely loved the Army but seeing Olivia there made me think that in our year apart Olivia had progressed to the Olympics and I hadn't! I had achieved much since the championships but this stirred me.

I thought to myself. I didn't regret joining the Army, that was what I had always wanted to do, but I might regret never trying to get into a boat for the London Olympics.

That was when I met Helen.

We had stayed in Bath whilst the others went on the camp and I remember it was a really cold winter. Neither of us wanted to go out on the water individually so we asked if we could go out in a double. We did and the rest is history.

Since 2010 we trained together pretty much every day without fail and two years later Helen and I won the first gold medal of the 2012 London Olympic and Paralympic Games.

In retrospect it is quite funny how Helen and I have different motivations for coming into the sport of rowing, though both of us relatively late on. Helen, because she wanted to win an Olympic gold and me because I wanted a socially good time! Yes, I changed my parameters quite quickly when I realised that rowing was actually a great sport and one that I was pretty good at. Very easily I could have picked another sport!

The three of us were then told we would be receiving MBEs. For me it was exciting and it was unexpected and it felt only right to be awarded the medals together. I was so proud.

The Queen started her chat with humour which I found both funny and surprising. I remember exactly what she said to us...

WHAT THE QUEEN SAID TO US...

"I see you two are still talking then!?"

Caught by surprise, for the first few seconds we were just laughing with The Queen of England! Pulling myself together I spoke first with "Yes. We do spend a lot of time together but thankfully we are still talking and still friends."

She continued by saying:

"Well, even better than that, you must feel great that your coach is going to be recognised later on today."

I think we both spoke after this comment. "Yes, we very much appreciate Robin being recognised. He deserves it and it's really important to us that we share this day together, after all we are a team."

The Queen asked Heather about going off to Afghanistan and me about my training for the World Championships in South Korea. She finished by saying she could see our rowing careers were still going very well. It did seem like quite a long chat which I enjoyed immensely and worth every second.

It was astounding to me. The Queen knew everything, she wasn't being briefed or told anything in her ear, she just had this very natural way of talking and we were with her for quite a while. She actually saw many people before she was briefed again. Clearly she has a remarkable memory. And the fact she opened with a joke was truly great.

Helen, Heather and Robin (Intersport Images Rowing)

Helen, Heather and Robin outside Buckingham Palace on the day of their investiture

SUM UP THE QUEEN IN ONE PARAGRAPH:

"*An amazing role model, ambassador and symbol of Great Britain for everyone. She is someone who has dedicated her life to serving our nation and still doing it at an age when most people want to sit with their feet up. I think The Queen is just incredible. I mean, she didn't choose to do the job and she wasn't even born to do it, but she took it on with open arms. Warm and genuine, I felt like she genuinely cared.*" – Helen

"*I thought The Queen was kind. For someone who meets so many people, she was interested. It was not a boring part of her day job and we were both really quite touched at how she seemed to enjoy the interaction. I never got the impression she was doing it because she felt duty bound. It was a nice moment for everyone, including Her Majesty I think. For each person to come away feeling like they had a unique interaction with her is something. Each person got something from it but equally I felt The Queen did too and seemed to be a happy, willing and wanting participant. That was a nice feeling.*" – Heather